Stitch, Spritz & Sew™

Curved Piecing As Easy As 1-2-3

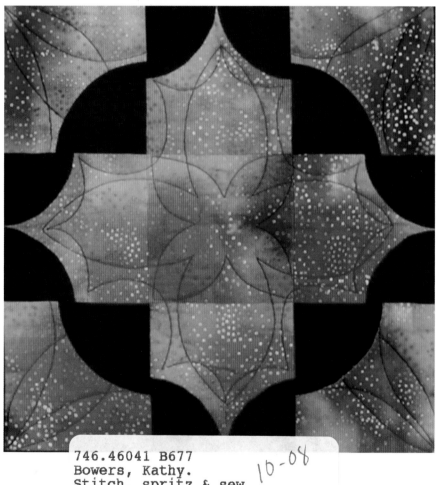

Kathy Bowers

Published by

krause publications

An Imprint of F+W Publications

700 East State Street • Iola, WI 54990-0001
715-445-2214 • 888-457-2873
www.krausebooks.com

Our toll-free number to place an order or obtain

a free catalog is (800) 258-0929.

The following registered trademark terms and companies appear in this publication:

Olfa, YLI Wash-A-Way, DMC, Kai, Beacon's Quilter's Choice Basting Glue,

Magic Sizing Fabric Finish, Gingher, Proctor Silex Steam Elite, Baby Lock,

Sulky, Madeira, WonderFil, and Husqvarna Viking.

Library of Congress Control Number: 2007942699

ISBN-13: 978-0-89689-578-2

ISBN-10: 0-89689-578-5

Designed by Heidi Bittner-Zastrow

Edited by Andy Belmas

Printed in Singapore

Dedication

I dedicate this book to the two guys in my life, my husband Jim, who has supported me whole heartedly through my many quilting endeavors and my grandson Matthew, who, as he puts it, was my sidekick while I made several of the quilts for the book. At age five, he clipped threads, punched buttons on the sewing machine, helped sew, and even pressed some blocks. And he was a good gofer when I needed something across the room. A big thanks to you both.

Acknowledgments

Many thanks to Andy Belmas, my editor, who gave me encouragement and guidance when I needed it most.

Thanks to my family and many friends who cheered me on when I felt overwhelmed by the whole book writing process with the mantra, "You can do this!" Special thanks to my Mom-in-Law Gertrude Bowers for her support and her telling me, "You better get back to work on the book." Without her, I might not have met my deadline.

Thanks to Johanne Moore for making and quilting Harlequin and for quilting Liberty Twist. Thanks to Debbie Short for quilting Just Ducky, Jack's Out of the Box, and Matthew's Quilt. Last, but not least, thanks to Danetta Burnett for quilting Meloncholy and Spinning Stars. You all are very talented quilters and wonderful friends; I would not have succeeded without your help and support.

Thanks to Moda Fabrics for supplying the beautiful fabric used in Meloncholy. And thanks to YLI and Superior Threads for providing such lovely threads used on quilts in the book.

Contents

7 Getting Started

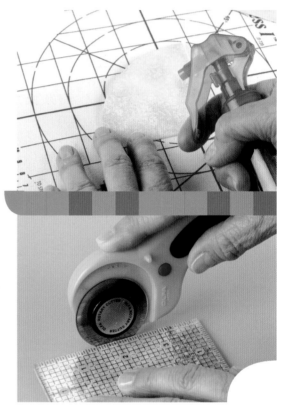

22 Basic Frame Instructions

44 Basic Arc Instructions

112 Basic Melon Instructions

124 Templates

127 Resources

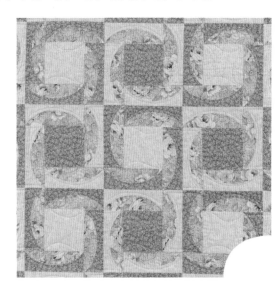

Introduction

My method for making curve-pieced quilts is fast, easy, and promises quick results. Just following my clear instructions to take your average quilt blocks, embroideries, or other textile artwork from the ordinary to extraordinary. You will need a few basic sewing supplies plus a few unconventional ones, too.

Standard needle-turn appliqué, for me, takes too long; and fusibles can be stiff and result in unwanted effects. So, I started adapting shapes that were mirror images to the reverse appliqué method and sewed them by machine with a secret ingredient: water-soluble thread.

The projects in this book progress from basic to more challenging, based on the piecing difficulty. Whether you are new to quilting or experienced, please take the time to make the sample heart shape. It will help you better understand inward and outward points as well as working with curves in a new way. Once you've used my easy construction method to make the heart frame—which, by the way, can be your first project or a project label—you'll be ready to move on to one of the many easy or challenging projects.

Pieced blocks start by making individual segments, which are combined to make pieced units, which are then joined to make blocks for the quilts featured in this book. There's no complicated math involved, but to better understand this method, it is essential to review the construction steps for each project before you begin.

In this book, you will find simple projects to get you started along with more challenging ones to jump-start your creativity. I'll share my excitement in creating reverse appliqué frames, arcs, melons, and labels the quick and easy way—by machine. Before long, you will be hooked on this easy method. Just be forewarned, this method can be addictive.

Happy stitching, and don't lick the thread!

Kathy Bowers

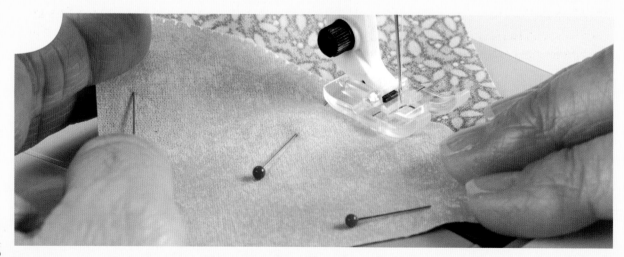

Getting Started

Tools

We quilters, like dressmakers, have a variety of tools we cannot live with out. There are a few necessities for the Stitch, Spritz, and Sew technique, and then there are the basics that are needed for quilting in general.

Necessities:
- Water-soluble thread (several brands are available; I prefer YLI Wash-A-Way)
- 50-wt. cotton thread (many brands are available; I prefer DMC 50-wt cotton or YLI Silk)
- Spray sizing
- Pinking shears (several brands are available; I prefer Kai because they cut to the tip)
- Fine-mist spray bottle
- Tracing paper
- Sixth finger stiletto (a pressing and sewing tool)
- A small hammer
- Glass-head fine pins (1⅜")
- Fabric glue with fine-tip applicator

Basics:
- Sewing machine in good working order
- Cotton or cotton/polyester piecing thread
- Size 60/8 or 70/10 universal machine needles
- Utility scissors for cutting paper or template plastic
- Iron and pressing board
- Template plastic (optional)
- Rotary cutter, mat, and rulers

It's hard to be specific about what rulers to use; I prefer to use the smallest ruler to get the job done. A smaller ruler is easier to hold in place when cutting, larger rulers can slip and cause a mis-cut. If you are going to purchase rulers, these are what I would recommend: 4", 6½", and 12½" squares (larger squares are helpful for larger blocks), 4" x 8", 6" x 12", and a 6" x 24". These allow a progression of sizing for easier of cutting of strips, blocks, and block segments.

Fabric

Select high-quality, 100% cotton fabrics. The big question "to wash or not to wash" can be a difficult question to answer. There are many views on this subject. I, for one, rely on sight and feel. If a fabric is stiff and the pigment used to color the fabric crocks (rubs off), I will usually leave it at the store. Should it make it home, it can take several washings to remove excess dye or pigment before the fabric is safe to put in a quilt.

Most current high-quality fabric manufacturers process their fabrics so bleeding is somewhat a thing of the past. As a safety precaution, I will usually wash most all reds and dark greens; because I have had problems with dye migration in those colors. A good rule to follow is, when in doubt, wash.

The next thing to consider is how the project will be used. If the quilt will be washed frequently, such as a baby quilt, I will definitely pre-wash the fabrics. If the project is a wall hanging, which may never be washed and only vacuumed now and then, I probably won't pre-wash the fabric.

Lastly, fabric that has been pre-washed tends to be somewhat limp because the filers put in by the manufacturer went down the drain when laundered. For this technique, putting a bit of body back into the fabric is a must. When I first started working with this appliqué process, I sprayed the individual pieces with spray sizing. However, if the pieces were small, they sometimes would stick to the bottom of the iron, and the ironing surface would be stained from sizing build up. For general ease of construction, I started pressing the pre-washed or un-washed fabric as a larger piece with the spray sizing. Then during construction, spritzing the block segments with water will reactivate the spray sizing, helping to keep seam allowances in place for the appliqué process.

Thread

Years ago, the only threads available for quilting were cotton or cotton wrapped polyester. Then, with the advent of embroidery machines, thread manufacturers began creating a wide variety of threads. As Bob Purcell, Father Superior of Superior Threads would say, "Good quality thread comes with a guarantee."

A quality thread will have less lint and require minimal machine adjustments. Select a high-quality cotton or cotton polyester thread intended for your application. A lingering question people have is, "Will polyester thread, if used in my quilt, cut the cotton fabric?" The answer is no; polyester thread will not cut through the fabric when used for either piecing or quilting. In the garment industry, a lot of cotton clothing is assembled with polyester or cotton polyester thread and I have yet to find my clothing falling apart from any breakage.

In recent years, the market place has come alive with so many thread choices. There is thread for every purpose, from basic piecing to embellishing. Unique and unusual threads can be used for quilting or surface embellishment on a quilt. However, I would suggest testing

Stitches

any threads you have in mind on scraps of your project fabric, batting, and backing. Things we think might work or look wonderful may not in application. I, for one, prefer to sew, not un-sew, and testing can prevent that unpleasant task.

In today's marketplace, we as quilters have a huge selection from which to choose. I have found that for piecing, a good cotton or cotton polyester are good choices. However, for the actual appliqué process, I prefer a 50-wt. cotton thread. The finer thread literally hides the machine stitches.

Select threads to complement or contrast with your project, and give a few of the amazing new threads on the market a try. Be creative and by all means have fun.

It is important to find a water-soluble thread that will release easily with a spritz of water and a press with a warm iron. Many brands are available, but some that I have tried require complete immersion in water to release, which is not an option for this technique. I prefer YLI Wash-A-Way. Should you find another brand that works, please relay that information. I would really like to know.

As there are many threads to choose from, there are a magnitude of stitches on the newer sewing machines to consider as well. With that said, I prefer using a simple pin stitch to sew appliqué segments to base units. As shown in the illustration below, the pin stitch is simply two stitches forward and one stitch swung to the left and back; then two more stitches forward and so on. Strive for a needle swing of 1.0 mm; the smaller the swing the less noticeable the stitches will be. That is very short and may take some practice to achieve. Until then, start with a 1.5-mm or 2.0-mm stitch width and a 2.5-mm or 3.0-mm stitch length.

Pin stitch

All is not lost if your machine is not equipped with a pin stitch or blanket stitch. If that's the case, you can use a narrow zigzag stitch—just be sure to match the thread as closely as possible to the appliqué fabric or use a monofilament thread to make the stitches less visible.

Blind hemstitch

A blind hemstitch is available on most machines, it provides an anchoring stitch. Again with this stitch, I would use monofilament thread to make the stitches invisible.

Zigzag stitch

I would avoid a straight stitch, because it is very difficult to straight stitch evenly along curved edges. I cannot stress enough the need to test, test, test your stitch and thread choices on scraps of project fabric until you achieve what looks best with your project.

Lastly, the stitch width and length noted here are what I have found works best for me and my machine. Strive for what works for you and your machine.

Straight Borders

Straight border strips can be cut on either the lengthwise or crosswise grain of the fabric. For large quilts, cross-grain pieces will need to be seamed together to make one long strip.

1 Measure the length of the quilt in two places and write the numbers down. If the two numbers are different, average them.

> **TIP**
>
> *Borders made from the lengthwise grain of fabric are easier to apply and they hang better, especially for wall hangings.*

2 Cut two side-border pieces to the length measurement. Piece strips as needed to meet this measurement. To piece strips, sew a diagonal seam, trim the excess, and press open.

3 Fold each border length (or unit) in half to find the center and mark with a pin or marking pencil. Next, find the centers of each side of the quilt and mark. With right sides together, pin borders to the sides of the quilt top. Match centering marks, and ease in any fullness. Sew each border in place. Press seams towards the border, unless instructed otherwise.

4 Next, measure the width of the quilt in two places, including the side borders. Write the numbers down and average them if they are different. Cut two border strips to this measurement. Repeat step three—finding centers, pinning, and stitching border strips in place on top and bottom. Press seams toward the border.

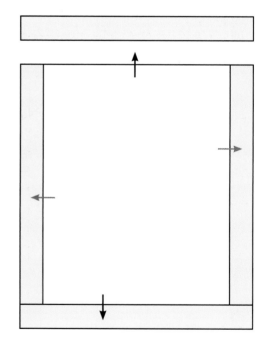

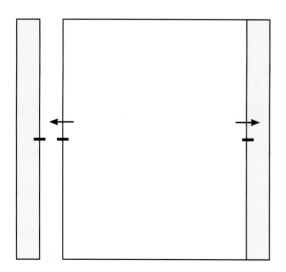

Mitered Borders

Mitered corners may be a little more difficult, but they add an attractive and elegant finish that is well worth the effort. Mitered borders are especially helpful when multiple borders are stitched together and treated as one unit.

1 First, assemble the border strips or units as indicated in the project instructions. To join the border strips, mark and stitch with a diagonal seam with right sides together. Add the number of strips to make the required length for your project.

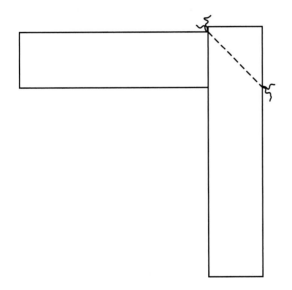

2 Measure your quilt in two places along the length. Write the numbers down. If the two numbers are different, find their average. Next, measure across the width in two places, writing the numbers down and averaging if necessary.

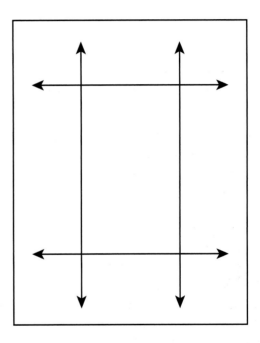

TIP

If the numbers are off more than ¼", it may be necessary to square your top before continuing. To square your quilt, work your way around the quilt's outer edge aligning a ruler with the same segment or unit. Use a rotary cutter to trim any irregularities outside the ruler's edge.

3 To length and width measurements, add two border widths and four extra inches. As an example, let's look at a quilt that measures 30" x 50" with 3"-wide borders. Cut two strips 40" long for the top and bottom borders and two 60" strips for the side borders.

Example:
30" + 3" + 3" + 4" = 40" top/bottom
50" + 3" + 3" + 4" = 60" sides

4 Fold border pieces (or units) in half and mark the centers with a pin or marking pencil. Find the centers of the sides of your quilt by folding it in half lengthwise and widthwise. Mark each center with a pin or marking pencil.

5 At each corner of the quilt top, mark a dot ¼" in from both edges.

TIP

Folding the whole quilt in quarters will not give you an accurate measurement due to the multiple layers at the folds.

6 Since extra inches were added to the border pieces to allow for the mitering process, measure and mark the actual width and length of each border before applying to the quilt.

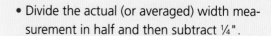
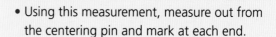

- Divide the actual (or averaged) width measurement in half and then subtract ¼".

- Using this measurement, measure out from the centering pin and mark at each end.

- Your mark should rest at the previously marked ¼" dot at the corners.

- Pin at center and each end, ease in any slight fullness as necessary while pinning the borders in place.

- Should there be more than ½" of fullness, re-measure the border. The strip may have been cut inaccurately or the quilt may have been measured inaccurately.

7 Stitch top border to quilt, backstitching at each end leaving ¼" unstitched. Repeat with the bottom and side border pieces. Press seam allowances toward the borders.

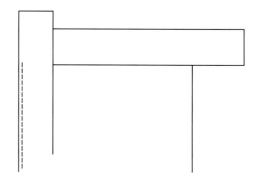
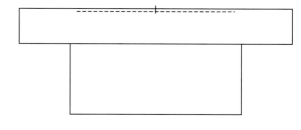

8 With one corner facing towards you, smooth it out so it is nice and flat. Extend left excess border end over right excess border end.

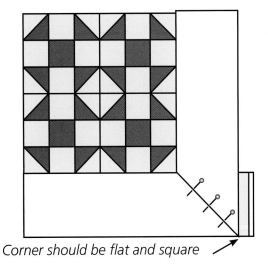

Corner should be flat and square

- Lift the left end with your right hand; place the pointer finger of your left hand where the borders meet at the quilt corner, so you can hold the quilt still.

- Turn the left end under and align the edges and any other border seams with those on the right border edge that is laying flat. Right sides will be facing.

- Carefully pin the edges that extend toward you. Press a crease along the miter edge. For multiple borders, place a pin at any intersecting border seams, matching seam lines. Once pressed, remove the pins that were holding the seams in place and leave the rest.

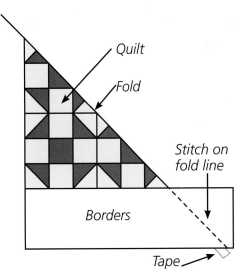

Quilt

Fold

Stitch on fold line

Borders

Tape

9 Now, lift the border and fold the quilt back, meeting the right sides of the quilt and the border edges. Pin them together securely.

10 Repeat with remaining three corners.

- Take the quilt top to the sewing machine and sew on the creased line.

- Remove the pins and lay the quilt out so you can check to see that the miter lays flat before you trim the seam allowance to ³⁄₈". Press the seam open or to one side. Should things not be to your liking, un-sew, reposition, and re-stitch before trimming.

TIP

To prevent mitered corners from stretching out of shape during quilting, apply a ³⁄₈" wide strip of self-adhesive stay tape the length of the miter seam. Center stay tape on the wrong side, over the ³⁄₈" seam allowance of each mitered corner and press in place.

Layering Your Quilt

Layering a quilt (the quilt sandwich) consists of three layers: the quilt top, the batting and the backing. For quilts wider than 42", the back will need to be pieced. Selvages shrink at a different rate than the pieced portion of the quilt top, so it is important to remove the selvage edges before seaming the backing pieces together.

Before measuring and piecing the backing, it may be helpful to square the top. Why would this be necessary? The quilt top can become uneven along the outer edges during construction, especially when pressed with steam.

To square the quilt, use a square and long ruler. Start by selecting a design element that you can follow all the way around the whole quilt, such as where blocks are joined. Align the square with the design element at the corner; note any unevenness outside the edge of the ruler, trim along both edges of the square ruler. Work your way around the quilt using the square and longer ruler.

1 To construct the backing for a quilt, measure the width and length of your finished quilt, add 2 to 4 extra inches to these measurements. Professional longarm quilters prefer that backings be at least 4 to 6 inches larger on all sides. For larger quilts, it may be necessary to cut and piece the backing in two or three sections. Cut and seam backing sections.

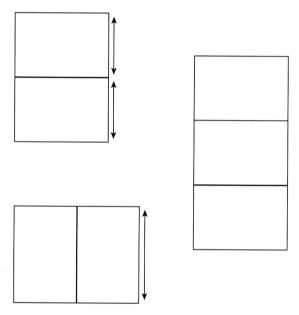

2 Carefully remove any loose threads from the back of the quilt and press.

3 Cut the batting one or two inches larger than the quilt top on all sides.

4 To find centers of quilt sides fold the top in half with edges even, place a pin or mark with a marking pencil. Refold the opposite direction and place a pin or mark these folds. Repeat this process with the backing as well, finding the centers and mark.

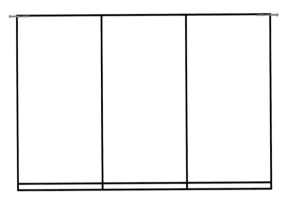

Pins mark the centers of the quilt sides.

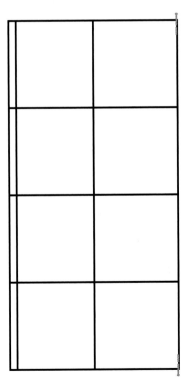

5 Tape backing to large work surface, right side facing down. Starting taping at the top centering pin, then tape at the center bottom pin, next to the center pins on each side. Work you way around the quilt taping across from previously taped area. Tape backing so it is taunt by not stretched, when you place your had in the center there shouldn't be any movement.

Lay batting over the backing centering and soothing it out. Batting should be slightly smaller than the backing so you can see the backing centering pins.

Next, lay the quilt top right side up over the batting, lining up the pins you placed at the folds on the top with those on the backing, smooth the top out being careful not to move the batting creating wrinkles.

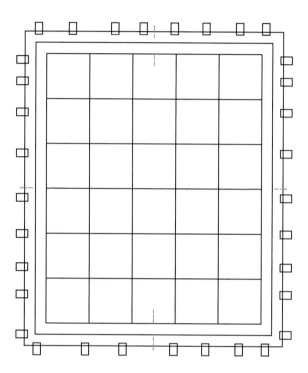

6 At this point for hand quilting, thread baste thru all layers in a grid pattern, taking long baste stitches.

For machine quilting, place quilters' 1" rust-proof safety pins every four to six inches apart. Preferably in areas out of the way for your quilting, insert all the pins then go back and close them using a pin-closing tool or grapefruit spoon.

Quilt according to specific pattern diagram or quilt design of choice.

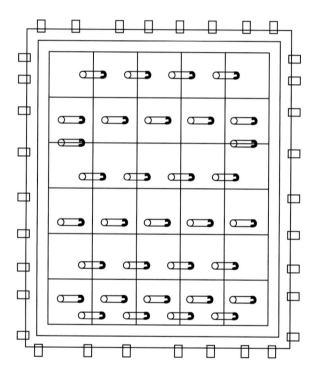

Quilt Labels

Years ago, quilt makers did not label their quilts. It's a shame they didn't leave quilt history for the generations that followed. For our future generations it is important that we quilters make labels for our quilts. Include the quilt's name if it has one, your name, where you lived when you made it, and the year. Also, if you took the top to someone else to be quilted, include her name, too.

For many of my quilts, I will take a design element from the quilt top and use it for the label. Even though it may need to be resized, the label will complement what is happening on the front of the quilt.

The label for Matthew's Quilt was just a square in a square block duplicating the yellow center and red triangle corners. For Jack's Out of the Box, I used four dark blue arcs and arranged them on a light blue base square, then entered the information in a unique way. The label is the last creative thing you can do to your quilt—make it something fun.

1 To make a frame-style label, follow the Basic Frame Instructions on page 22. Cut the frame fabric square an inch or so bigger than your desired finished size so you can trim it when it is complete.

2 For the best visibility of label information, choose a light-colored base fabric—white or cream muslin are good choices. Another option is to make the label center portion from the lightest fabric color in the quilt top, as long as the words can be read easily.

3 With a black pen or permanent marker, draw lines ¼" to ⅜" apart on the paper side of a piece of freezer paper cut a little larger than your label opening. The lines need to be dark enough to be visible through the fabric (or use a light box). The lines will be your guide for entering the quilt information on the label base fabric.

> ### TIP
> *Make the label as a unit. Do not stitch the label frame in place on the base fabric until the quilt information has been written on it. If there are any mistakes, it is easier to replace the base fabric than it is to remake the frame.*

4 Now that everything is ready, center and press the shiny side of the lined freezer paper to the wrong side of the base fabric. Then, with the base fabric right side up, center the label frame over the base fabric. Pin in a few places to secure (do not stitch together yet). With a Pigma pen or other fabric-safe permanent pen, write your quilt information, using the lined freezer paper as your guide.

5 Carefully remove the freezer paper and stitch the frame to the base fabric. Review step 15 in Basic Frame Instructions for stitching and machine setup information.

6 Trim the extra base fabric away from the backside, and then trim the outer frame edges to the desired size. Turn the top and right side edges under ¼" and press, apply to the lower left corner of the quilt back. Next, hand stitch the top and right edge of the label to the quilt. Then finish by turning the binding over the bottom and left edges of the label. Hand stitch the balance of the binding in place.

TIP

To make hand sewing the label on your quilt easier, first pin the label in place. With your needle and thread, start stitching at the bottom right corner of the label. With the edge of the quilt label laying over the edge of your work surface, take your first stitch into the backing fabric, now tilt the needle's eye end down and catch the edge of the label. By keeping the quilt over the edge of your work surface as you work, you will not have to bunch up the quilt or be stuck by pins.

Hanging Sleeve

A hanging sleeve is a tube of fabric that is sewn to the back of a quilt. A dowel or rod placed thru the sleeve to hang it from a quilt shelf or at a quilt show, where a sleeve is usually required. A good time to add the sleeve is when the binding is being attached, to conceal the raw edges. Make the sleeve from the project backing fabric or other fabric such as muslin.

1 Measure the side of your quilt where the sleeve is to be applied. Cut a strip of fabric 6" wide by this measurement. For large quilts, it may be necessary to piece one or more pieces together to equal the required length.

2 Fold the short ends to the wrong side ⅜" then fold one more time, press then stitch in place.

3 Fold in half lengthwise with wrong sides together, press along fold.

4 Place sleeve on the back of the quilt meeting raw edges of the sleeve with the raw edges of the quilt top, pin in place.

5 Stitch sleeve to the edge of the quilt, seam line should be shy of the ¼" seam allowance.

6 Hand stitch the fold edge to the quilt taking care to catch only the backing with your stitches.

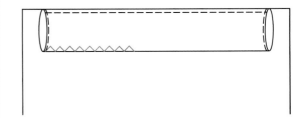

7 Finish by folding binding to the back of the quilt concealing the raw edges and slipstitch binding in place.

Binding

Once your project is quilted, the next step is to bind the edges. The numbers of binding strips needed for the projects in this book are provided in the cutting directions at the beginning of each project.

1 Join binding strips with right sides together, mark and stitch with a diagonal/miter seam. Add number of strips to make one long piece.

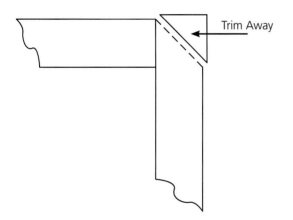

Trim Away

2 Trim each diagonal seam allowance to ¼", press seam open.

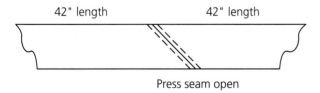

42" length   42" length

Press seam open

3 Press binding in half lengthwise with wrong sides together.

> **TIP**
>
> *A walking foot is helpful to apply the binding; it keeps the layers from shifting as the binding is stitched in place.*

> **TIP**
>
> *Before stitching the binding in place, first lay the completed binding around the edge of the quilt adjusting as necessary so a diagonal seam does not fall directly on a corner.*

4 Before applying the binding to your quilt, it is a good practice to square the top. Work your way around the quilts outer edges aligning a long ruler for the sides and a large square at the corners with the same block segment or unit, trim any irregularities outside the rulers' edge.

5 Leave eight to ten inches of the binding free; start stitching the binding to the quilt in the middle of any side using a ¼" seam allowance. Stop stitching ¼" away from the corner, pivot with the needle down and stitch at an angle to the point of the corner, cut thread.

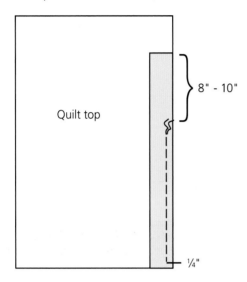

6 Fold binding up and then back down even with the edge of the quilt. Continue stitching where the previous stitching ended, stitching the binding to the outer edge of the quilt, repeat at each corner.

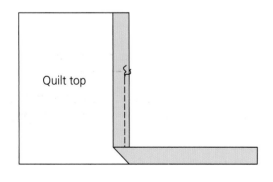

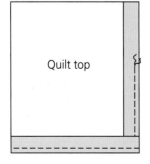

7 Stop stitching and backstitch 8" to 12" from where you started stitching. Remove quilt from sewing machine.

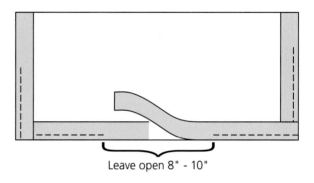

Leave open 8" - 10"

8 On your work surface, place the bulk of the quilt away from you. Smooth the starting end so it is nice and flat and pin to the quilt in a couple of places to secure. Overlap the end tail over the start tail and trim overlap at 2½".

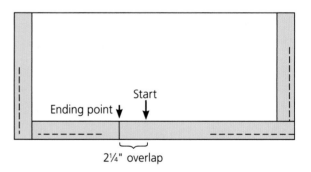

2¼" overlap

9 In your left hand open the start tail so the right side is facing you. In your right hand, open the end tail so the wrong side is facing you. Over lap the ends at a right angle and right sides together. Secure with pins and mark a diagonal stitching line.

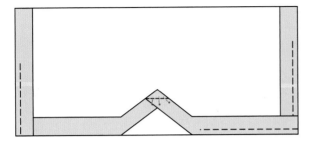

10 Stitch on the marked line, before trimming excess check to see that you have stitched correctly and that binding lays evenly, if not, unpick and stitch again. When you are happy with the results, trim seam allowance to ¼", open and finger press seam. Refold binding, reposition on edge and finish stitching binding to quilt.

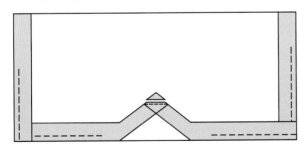

11 Fold binding over raw edges to back of quilt, blind stitch to secure binding in place by hand. As the binding is worked around the quilt, a miter will form at the corners; tack the miter fold with a few stitches before continuing.

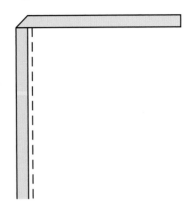

12 Add label prior to stitching the binding in place at the lower left corner on the backside of the quilt.

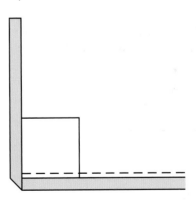

13 A hanging sleeve can also be added to the quilt back at the top for wall hangings prior to securing the binding in place.

TIP

I will usually insert the quilt label under the binding at the lower left corner of the quilt back, including the label under the binding as I hand stitch it in place.

Basic Frame Instructions

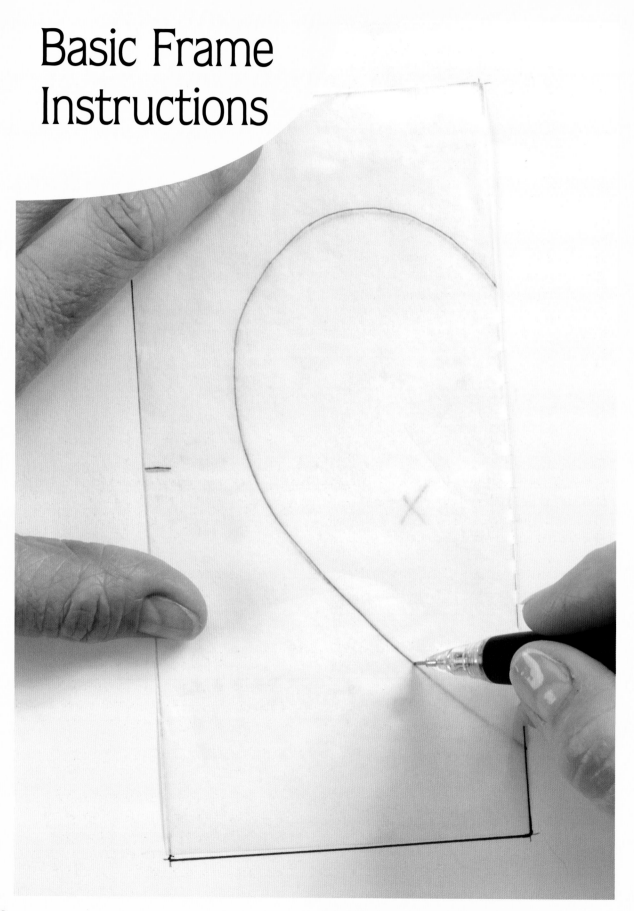

My first experience with this technique was making a frame for a snowman block exchange. The machine-embroidered snowmen were nice but needed something to set them off. After a bit of experimenting the frame was born, and, as they say, the rest is history.

Frames can create a unique block or enhance a simple block. They can frame a piece of embroidery, a photo transfer, or a panel print. The keys to this technique are using water-soluble thread and working with a frame that is a mirror image (in which both halves are identical).

The first frame project—the heart frame—will help you understand inward and outward points. Once you master the heart frame, you will be well on your way to creating unique blocks and quilts.

Frame Construction

1 Press frame fabric well with spray sizing prior to cutting. Spray sizing gives fabric firmness as well as a nice, crisp, turned-under seam edge in preparation for the appliqué process.

2 Cut desired size fabric square according to chosen project (for this sample, I cut the square to 6" x 6"). Note, squares are slightly oversized to allow for trimming when the frame is complete.

3 Frame projects are mirror-image shapes, which means both halves of the shape are identical. And, only half of the pattern is provided. As an example, we will use the heart label template from page 125. Trace the heart shape onto

> **TIP**
>
> *Feel free to enlarge or reduce the heart patterns to fit your needs. However, in doing so, you would also need to make other pattern adjustments.*

Heart Label

> **TIP**
>
> *I use exam-table paper for patterns, templates, and designing. It is sturdy, thin enough to see through, and very inexpensive. It is available at many medical supply stores or can be mail ordered (see Resources on page 127). Be sure to purchase the smooth style.*

tracing paper or exam-table tissue paper, along with the one registration mark. Then trim the center portion of the pattern away.

4 To set up your machine, place water-soluble thread in the bobbin and regular thread in the top. Insert a new size 70/10 universal needle. If you experience skipped stitches, change to a larger 80/12 universal needle.

> **TIP**
>
> *Should you choose to put the water-soluble thread in the needle, lower the upper tension two or three numbers and don't lick the thread when threading the needle!*

- When winding a bobbin with water-soluble thread, be sure to mark the bobbin so you won't mistake it for regular white thread.

- Remember to remove the water-soluble thread from your machine when template stitching is complete.

- Store the bobbin and the spool of water-soluble thread in a plastic bag with one of those silica packs found in vitamin bottles to keep it moisture free.

TIP

Some sewing machines have a problem with water-soluble thread in the top tension which causes thread breakage. Putting it in the bobbin eliminates problems.

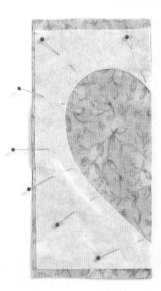

5 Fold frame fabric square in half with right sides together and edges even. Then fold it again into quarters. Mark the second fold with a pin or marking pencil. Pin the heart pattern to the first fold, aligning the heart center with the fold line and matching the registration mark on the heart template with the second fold mark. The registration mark helps to insure that the frame is centered on the fabric regardless of its size. The pattern remains in place until the stitching is complete. By placing the pins with the points towards the stitching line, the presser foot will glide over the pin-points, eliminating the need to remove them as you sew.

TIP

It is easier to start sewing at the bottom of the heart as opposed to the point end, where the pattern point has a tendency to flip back under the machine foot.

6 Stitch along the inner edge of the frame template using a stitch length of 2.0 mm or 14 stitches per inch. With a short stitch length, backstitching is not necessary.

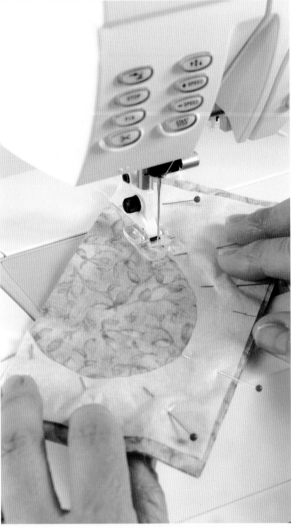

7 Remove the pattern and trim the center portion away with pinking shears, leaving a fat ⅛" seam allowance. Some curves may need an extra clip or two to prevent puckering once turned. At the bottom point of the heart, clip on the fold line, stopping a few threads short of the stitching.

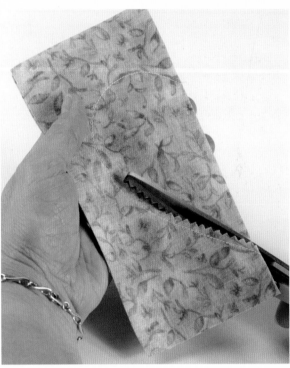

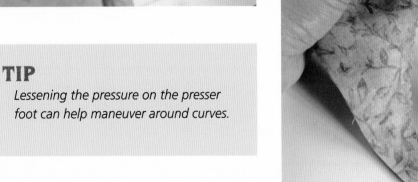

TIP

Lessening the pressure on the presser foot can help maneuver around curves.

TIP

I have found that an old machine needle is a good tool to nudge out points. It does not bend, and if you're careful, you will not accidentally pull out strands of the fabric as can happen using a straight pin.

8 From the right side, press the seam allowance to one side along the straight and curved seam lines with a fingernail or wooden iron. You will be amazed at how easy it is to achieve a crisp turned edge. Nudge the top point out the best you can; we will adjust the point in step eleven.

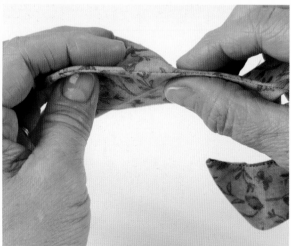

TIP

Fabric warmed with an iron will absorb water more easily than cool fabric.

9 Turn right side out, align raw edges, and press. Try not to press the remaining fold at the ends; doing so will put a crease in the frame edge. Spritz with a fine mist spray bottle, but go easy with the water—getting things too wet can cause the seam allowance to pop out and not stay put. Press the fabric dry, again being careful not to press creases at the fold ends. Gently tug at the seam to separate. If the water-soluble thread does not release easily, spritz, press dry, and try again. It may be helpful to have the water-soluble thread facing up when you begin.

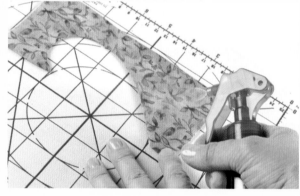

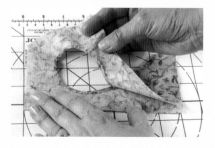

TIP

Should you find that your pieces are "shrinking" after you spritz and press them, you may want to pre-wash your fabrics. Shrinkage can be an issue with any pieced block. If you have been careful with cutting and seaming, and the blocks do not measure what the pattern calls for, shrinkage could be the problem.

10 Open the frame and lay it on your pressing surface seam side up. Carefully remove the regular thread, holding the seam allowance in place with your fingertips as you gently pull the thread out. Press the seam allowance and clip the bottom end of the heart a tad more if it won't lay flat on its own.

11 Now to the top point of the heart, which is a little trickier to re-press. Place the heart frame wrong side up on your pressing surface as shown. Carefully fold out the seam allowance at the point. Fold one edge back along the stitching line. Next, fold the other side back over the first, holding it with a pin so you can press it in place. Sometimes it is necessary to trim this last edge just a tad so it won't show from the right side.

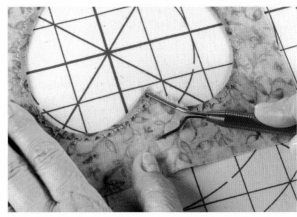

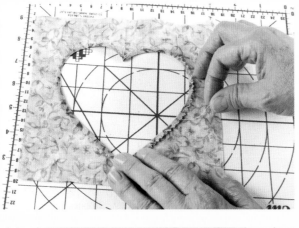

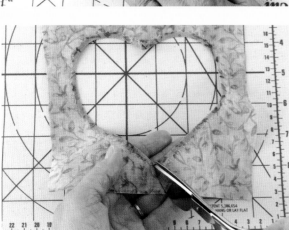

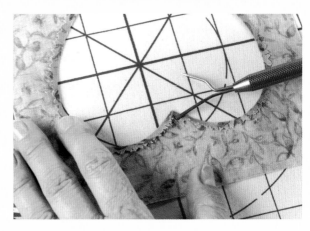

12 Turn the heart frame over, and give it a good press from the right side.

> **TIP**
>
> *Instead of focal fabric, you may want to place the frame around a photo, a piece of embroidery, or some other motif.*

13 Position the finished heart frame opening over the focal fabric, meeting the wrong side of the frame to the right side of the focal fabric. Allow excess base fabric to extend past the inner edge of the heart frame. (In this example, the base fabric is a simple contrasting print.)

14 Pin the heart frame to the base fabric as shown, placing the pins so the points are towards the heart center. Another option is to use fabric glue with a fine-tip applicator to adhere the layers together. The glue holds very well, takes about ten minutes to dry, and is water-soluble.

15 Use a pin stitch to stitch the frame in place as shown on page 29. The pin stitch is available on many newer sewing machines. It resembles a hand stitched blanket stitch. Match your thread color to the base fabric to hide any little wobbles as you learn to stitch in the ditch to appliqué the frame to the base fabric.

16 Turn the completed piece over so the back-side is up, and, using either pinking shears or appliqué scissors, carefully trim away the excess focal fabric along the inner edge of the frame. Be careful not to catch the frame as you trim.

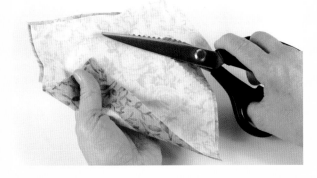

17 Using a rotary cutter, mat, and square ruler, trim and square the finished frame outer edges to the desired size.

- Test your thread and stitch choices on scraps of both appliqué and base fabric. Strive for a stitch length of 2.0 mm or 3.0 mm and a needle position of 1.0 mm. The needle position is the swing of the needle into the fabric; the smaller the swing the less noticeable these stitches will be.

- For future projects, once you feel comfortable stitching in the ditch to attach the appliqué to the base fabric, try matching the thread to the frame fabric. I have found that a finer 50-wt. cotton thread hides the stitches better. For finer threads, select a finer size 60/8 or 70/10 needle as well.

- If your machine does not have a pin or blanket stitch, use a narrow zigzag stitch. In this case, match the thread to the appliqué or use monofilament thread. A blind hemstitch can provide an anchoring stitch, but creates a "V" shaped stitch that may not be attractive. A straight stitch is not a good choice because it is very difficult to stitch an even line of stitches along straight or curved edges. No matter what stitch you choose, I cannot stress enough the need to test your stitch and thread choices on scraps of project fabrics.

- Frames can be constructed and appliquéd by hand, making the stitches invisible. Glue baste the layers together or place pins on the backside, which eliminates the possibility of catching the thread on the pins while hand stitching.

Sweet Hearts

Pieced and quilted by the author
Finished size: 16" x 38" • Block size: 10½" unfinished
Seam allowance: ¼"

This sweet little heart wall hanging can be small, or, by adding more blocks, can become a crib or bed quilt. No matter the size, this project is the perfect way to start your water-soluble thread adventure.

Materials

All calculations based on 42" fabric width.

- 2 yd. toile or other focal print for heart centers and backing
- 1 yd. blue for heart frames, nine patches, sashing, and binding
- ½ yd. white for nine patches and sashing
- 18" x 40" batting
- Heart Template

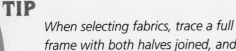

TIP

When selecting fabrics, trace a full frame with both halves joined, and trim out the center. Take the frame to the fabric store, and use the opening in the frame to audition focal fabrics for your project.

Cutting Instructions

Note: *For ease during construction, press all fabrics well with spray sizing prior to cutting strips.*

- **Blue**

    1 strip 11" x 42"; cut into three 11" x 11" squares

    5 strips 1½" x 42" wide for nine-patch units and sashing

    3 strips 2½" x 42" wide for binding

- **White**

    7 Strips 1½" x 42" wide for nine-patch units and sashing

Making the Frames

1 Trace the heart template from page 125 to pattern paper. Include the registration mark.

2 Fold an 11" square in half with the right sides together. Then fold one more time into quarters and mark the second fold. Unfold the second fold, and pin the heart template to the first fold. Align the heart center with the fold line, and align the registration mark on the template with the second fold mark.

3 Stitch along the inner edge of the heart template with water-soluble thread in either the bobbin or top tension. Trim the center portion away with pinking shears and turn right side out. Some tight curves and outward points may need a few clips to ensure they will not pucker once turned. Open the frame, referring to steps six through eleven of the Basic Frame Instructions on pages 25-27.

TIP

Pinking the seam edge with pinking shears allows for ease along the curve once the frame is turned right side out.

4 Repeat steps three and four with the remaining two blue 11" squares. You will end up creating three heart frames. Remove the water-soluble thread from your machine when template stitching is complete and store it properly.

Appliquéing the Frames

1 Carefully arrange heart frames over toile or other focal fabric until you have a pleasing arrangement. Whether you are pin basting or glue basting, be sure to allow enough base fabric to extend beyond the heart frame for basting. For basting details, refer to step fourteen on page 28 in Basic Frame Instructions.

2 Using a new 70/10 universal machine needle and a pin stitch or other decorative stitch, appliqué the heart frame to the toile base fabric.

3 Turn the finished heart block over and trim excess fabric from around the outer edge of the heart. Take care to avoid catching the frame fabric with shears while trimming. See step sixteen on page 29.

4 Press the finished blocks, and trim to 10½" x 10½" square. Refer to step seventeen on page 29.

Making the Nine-Patch Units and Sashing

1 Begin with your blue and white 1½" x 42" strips. Sew two white strips to either side of a blue strip. Press seams toward the blue. Make three. Sub-cut into ten 10½" x 3½" units and ten 1½" x 3½" units.

Make three sets.

2 With the remaining 1½" x 42" strips, sew two blue strips to either side of the white strip. Press seams toward to the blue. Sub-cut into sixteen 1½" x 3½" units.

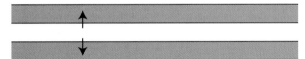

Make one set.

3 Assemble, stitch, and press nine-patch blocks as diagramed.

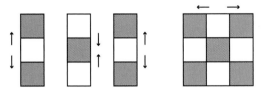

Quilt Top Assembly

1 Following the block layout diagram, arrange and sew the heart blocks, sashing, and nine-patch units together. Press as shown.

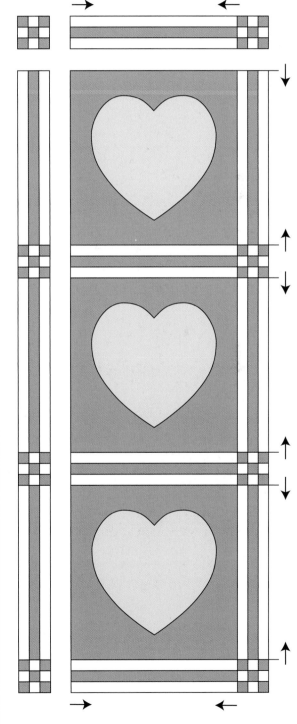

Finishing

1 To complete your quilt, first refer to Layering Your Quilt on page 14. Layer the quilt top with batting and backing, and pin or hand baste the layers together.

2 See the quilting diagram for quilting ideas or quilt as desired. Basic stitch-in-the-ditch quilting was done along all the straight seams and around the heart shape. Medium stipple was used on the blue frame with a limited amount of outline stitching on the toile motif center.

3 Assemble the binding using a diagonal seam, sewing three blue 2½" x 42" strips together. Refer to binding instructions on page 19.

4 Before stitching the binding in place, lay the long binding strip around the edge of the quilt. Adjust the strip as necessary so a diagonal seam does not fall directly on a corner.

5 Stitch the binding to the outer edge of the quilt, then turn to the back and hand stitch in place. Remember to label your quilt. Consider making a frame label as a unique finish to your quilt, label instructions can be found on page 17.

TIP

To make hand sewing the label on your quilt easier, first pin the label in place. With needle and thread, start stitching at the bottom right corner of the label. With the edge of the quilt label laying over the edge of your work surface, take your first stitch into the backing fabric. Now tilt the needle's eye end down and catch the edge of the label. By keeping the quilt over the edge of your work surface as you work, you will not have to bunch up the quilt or be stuck by pins.

Just Ducky

Pieced by the author; quilted by Debbie Short
Finished size: 36" x 36" • Block size: 8½" unfinished
Seam allowance: ¼"

This wall hanging is a fun way to try your hand at the frame technique. It is the perfect gift for a new mom. Or you can change the focal fabric for a whole new look. Frames are a versatile design element that can be adapted to a variety of projects.

Materials

All calculations based on 42" fabric width.

- ½ yd. print focal fabric for frame centers (check that you have 9 full motifs)
- 1½ yd. blue
- ½ yd. red for sashing and inner border
- 4 coordinating fat quarters
- 40" x 40" batting
- Just Ducky Template

TIP

To audition fabrics for the center of the frame, trace a full frame for the project on tissue paper and trim out the center. Take the frame to the fabric store and use the opening in the frame to audition focal fabrics for your project.

Cutting Instructions

Note: *For easier construction, press all fabrics well with spray sizing prior to cutting strips.*

- **Blue**

  3 strips 10" x 42"; cut into nine squares, 10" x 10" for frames

  1 strip 2½" x 42"; cut into sixteen squares, 2½" x 2½" for corner stones

  4 strips 2½" x 42" for outer border

  4 strips 2½" x 42" for binding

- **Red**

  1 strip 8½" x 42"; cut into 12 rectangles, 2½" x 8½" for sashing

  1 strip 2" x 42"; cut into 12 rectangles, 2" x 2½" for inner border units

- **Fat Quarters**

  Cut two 2" x 22" strips from each fat quarter, cut into 12 rectangles 2" x 2½" for inner border units

TIP

I have found that rectangles cut with the lengthwise grain press straighter, have less stretch, and ravel less. Try it.

Making the Frames

1 Trace the Just Ducky template from page 125 on to tracing paper. Be sure to include the registration mark.

2 Fold a 10" square in half with the right sides facing. Then fold one more time into quarters and mark the second fold. Unfold the second fold and pin the frame template to the first fold. Align the heart center with the fold line, and align the registration mark on the template with the second fold mark. The registration mark will help you center your template on the fabric regardless of its size.

3 Stitch along the inner edge of the frame template with water-soluble thread. Trim the center portion away with pinking shears and turn right side out. Some tight curves may need a few clips to ensure they will not pucker once turned. Follow steps six through ten on pages 25-27. Press and open frame.

4 Repeat step three with remaining eight blue squares, creating nine frames in all. Remove water-soluble thread from the machine when your template stitching is complete.

> **TIP**
>
> *Fabric warmed with an iron will absorb water more easily than cool fabric.*

Appliqué Frame to Base Fabric

1 Carefully arrange the frames over your focal fabric until you have a pleasing arrangement. Be sure to allow enough base fabric to extend beyond the inner edge of the frame to pin or glue baste in place. For pinning details, refer to step fourteen on page 28.

2 Use a new 70/10 universal machine needle and a pin stitch to appliqué the frame to the base fabric. Always test your thread and stitch choices on scraps of your project fabric before you start.

3 Turn the finished frame over and trim the excess fabric from around the outer edge of the frame, taking care not to catch the frame fabric with shears. Press the finished blocks and trim to 8½" x 8½" square.

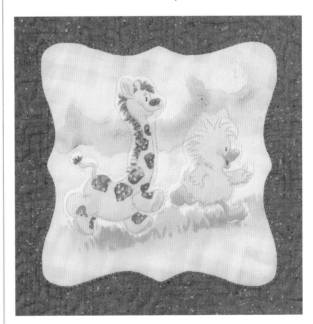

Quilt Top Assembly

1 Following the block layout diagram, arrange and sew the blocks, sashing, and pieced-border units together in vertical rows.

2 Before adding the borders, it is a good idea to square the top. Work your way around the quilt's outer edge, aligning a ruler with the same block segment or unit. With a rotary cutter, carefully trim any edge irregularities that extend outside the edge of the ruler.

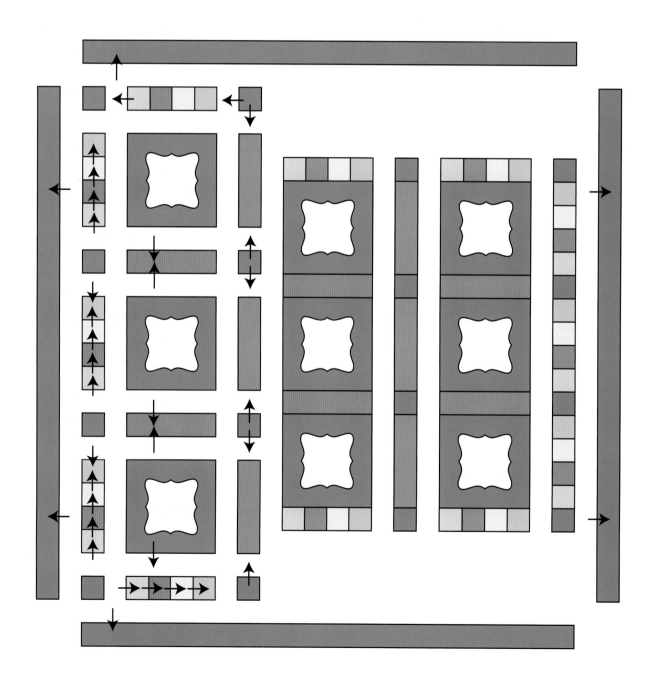

Pieced Border Assembly

1 Arrange the 2" x 2½" rectangles for the inner border, following the layout diagram. The arrangement can be organized or scrappy. Sew the rectangles together into four-rectangle units. Make twelve.

2 Join three of the rectangle units from step one with two blue 2" x 2½" rectangles to make an inner border strip. Make four. Add a blue 2" x 2½" rectangle to each end of two of the strips for the corners. See the layout diagram.

Border Assembly

1 Measure the squared quilt down its length in two or three places. Write down and average these measurements.

2 From two blue 2½" border strips, cut the two side borders to the measurements from step one.

3 Find the centers of the quilt and the side border pieces, and mark them with pins or a marking pencil. Align the centers of the long edges of the border with the quilt centers. Pin them in place and sew. Press seam allowances toward the outer border.

4 With the two remaining blue strips, repeat steps one through three for the top and bottom outer borders. Press the completed top and clip any loose threads.

Finishing

1 Refer to Layering Your Quilt instructions on page 14. Layer the quilt top with batting and backing, and baste the layers together.

2 Use the quilting design shown in the diagram or quilt as desired.

3 Assemble the binding by sewing three blue 2½" x 42" strips together using a diagonal seam. Refer to Binding on page 19.

4 Before stitching the binding in place, lay the completed binding around the edge of the quilt. Adjust as necessary so a diagonal seam does not fall directly on a corner.

5 Stitch the binding to the outer edge of the quilt; then turn to the back and hand stitch in place. Be sure to label your quilt. Consider making a frame label as a unique finish to your quilt. A sample label is found on page 17.

Fancy Frame Place Mats

Pieced and quilted by the author
Finished size: 13" x 19" place mats, 14½" x 14½" napkins
Seam allowance: ¼"

These lovely place mats will add a distinctive touch to your dining table or to that of a friend or relative. The napkins complete the setting, as the narrow binding complements the quilted project.

Materials

All calculations based on 42" fabric width.

- 3 yd. red floral print
- 1¾ yd. green tone-on-tone print
- Batting: four 13½" x 19½" cotton batting
- Fancy Frame Template

TIP

Use flannel instead of batting for a thinner feeling place mat.

Cutting Instructions

• **Red floral print**

4 strips 14" x 42"; cut into eight rectangles 14" x 20" for frame and backing pieces

2 strips 14½" x 42"; cut into four squares 14½" x 14½" for napkins

7 strips 2½" x 42" for place mat binding

• **Green tone-on-tone print**

2 strips 11" x 42"; cut into four rectangles 11" x 17" for frame centers

2 strips 14½" x 42"; cut into four squares 14½" x 14½" for napkins

6 strips 1½" x 42" for napkin binding

Making the Frames

Note: For ease of construction, press all fabrics well with spray sizing prior to cutting strips.

1 Trace the Place Mat Frame template from page 125 to tracing paper. Connect the two sections together at the dotted line.

2 Fold a 14" x 20" rectangle in half so the right sides are together and the 14" sides meet. Then, fold once more into quarters and mark the second fold with a pin or marking pencil. Unfold the second fold. Pin the frame template to the first fold, aligning the center cut out with the fold line and matching the registration mark on the template with the second fold mark. The registration mark will help you center your pattern on the fabric regardless of fabric size.

3 Stitch along the inner edge of the frame template with water-soluble thread in either the bobbin or top tension. Trim the center portion away with pinking shears and turn right side out. Some tight curves and outward points may need a few clips to ensure they will not pucker once they are turned. Open the frame, and finger press the seam allowance to one side. Refer to steps six through ten on pages 25-27.

> **TIP**
>
> *To help eliminate distortion when stitching, lessen the pressure on the presser foot. This will allow you to stitch along the curves more easily with minimal lifting of the presser foot.*

4 Repeat step three with the remaining three red floral 14" x 20" rectangles. Remove the water-soluble thread from the machine when the template stitching is complete.

Appliqué Frame to Base Fabric

1 Carefully center each red print frame over a green 11" x 17" base rectangle. The base fabric should extend evenly under the frame. Pin or glue baste in place.

2 Using a new 70/10 universal machine needle and a pin stitch or other decorative stitch, appliqué the frame to the base fabric. Always test your thread and stitch choices on scraps of your project fabric.

3 Turn the stitched frame over and trim the excess green base fabric from the inner edge of the frame. Take care not to catch the frame fabric with shears while trimming. Press the finished place mat, and trim to 14" x 20".

Finishing

1 Layer each place mat with batting and backing. Pin or hand baste the layers together. Refer to Layering Your Quilt on page 14 as needed.

2 The quilting used for the place mats is simply stitch-in-the-ditch along the inner frame edge, then again ½" away on either side of the first stitching. A medium stipple was stitched in the place mat center and outer frame. Or quilt as desired.

3 Trim the outer edges of the quilted place mats to 13" x 19".

Binding

1 Assemble the binding using a diagonal seam, sewing the seven red floral print 2½" x 42" strips together. Before stitching the binding to each place mat, lay the binding around the outer edge. Adjust as necessary so a diagonal seam does not fall directly on a corner.

2 Apply the binding to the front side of your place mats, stitching in place along the outer edges of each place mat. Join the ends. Turn the binding to the backside and hand stitch in place. Review Binding on page 19. Label your place mats if you choose.

Napkin Construction

Note: Batting and quilting stitches are not necessary to construct the napkins.

1 With wrong sides together, pin or lightly hand baste a green 14½" x 14½" square and a red floral print 14½" x 14½" square meeting wrong sides together.

2 To assemble the binding, sew six 1½" x 42" green strips together using a diagonal seam. As before, lay the binding around the edge, adjusting as necessary so a diagonal seam does not fall directly on a corner.

Note: The binding for the napkins is a single layer so there will be less bulk on the napkin's edge.

3 Machine stitch the binding to the red print side. Align the right side of the binding and its cut edge with the outer edge of each napkin. Join the ends, and turn the binding to the green side. Fold the raw edge under and hand stitch in place.

Basic Arc Instructions

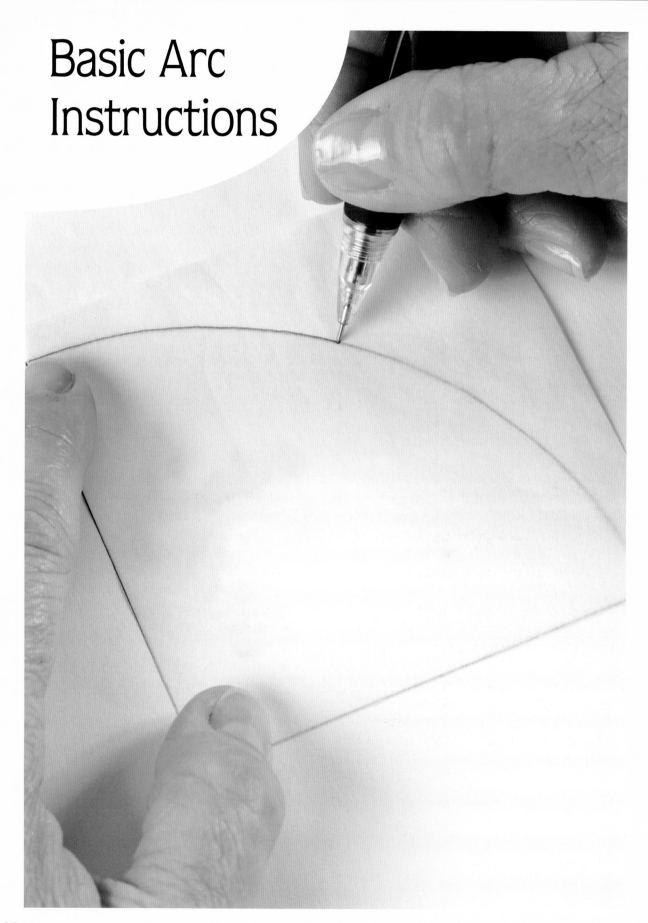

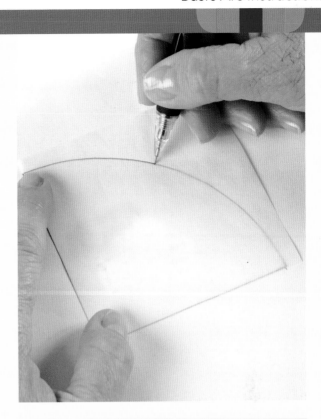

After my adventure with frames, the challenge was on to find other ways to use water-soluble thread. I had designed several interesting curved piece projects but really did not want to use the conventional method of sewing convex to concave pieces. Then the light bulb came on! Why not make the arcs first then apply them to squares, rectangles, or whatever base fabric I chose?

After I created a few projects using arcs, I began to look at conventional angled blocks and the "what if" thought came to mind. I began doodling on a few blocks, changed angled lines to arcs, and again "the rest is history."

Traditional curved piecing requires you to sew together a concave (curved-in) piece to a convex (curved-out) piece. This can be difficult for quilters of all skill levels. But the mirror-image curves (what I call arcs) that are presented in this chapter are a breeze.

Curve Construction

1 Press arc fabric well using spray sizing prior to cutting. Spray sizing gives fabric firmness as well as a nice crisp turned-under seam edge in preparation for the appliqué process.

2 Cut desired size fabric squares for chosen project. Trace the appropriate arc template from page 124 onto tracing paper.

3 Place water-soluble thread in the bobbin, regular thread in the top, and insert a new size 70/10 universal needle. If you experience skipped stitches, go to a larger 80/12 universal machine needle.

- Should you choose to put the water-soluble thread in the needle instead of in the bobbin, lower the upper tension two or three numbers and don't lick the thread when threading the needle.

- It's important to find a water-soluble thread that will release easily. I prefer YLI Wash-A-Way. Some brands may require complete immersion of your project in water to release, which is to be avoided.

- Be sure to mark the bobbin so you will not mistake the water-soluble thread for regular white thread.

- Remember to remove the water-soluble thread from your machine when template stitching is complete.

- Store the water-soluble thread bobbin and spool in a plastic bag with a silica pack found in vitamin bottles to keep it moisture free.

TIP

Some sewing machines have a problem with water-soluble thread in the top tension causing thread breakage. You can eliminates most problems by putting it in the bobbin.

4 Place two squares together with right sides facing and edges even. Pin an arc template to the squares. Place the pins with the points toward the stitching line.

TIP

To help eliminate distortion when stitching, I try to align the grain lines of the two squares. Lessening the pressure on the presser foot can help as well.

5 Stitch along the edge of the arc template using a stitch length of 2.0 mm or 14 stitches per inch and water-soluble thread. With a short stitch length, backstitching is not usually necessary. When creating arcs for a project, it is a good idea to pin several templates to several pairs of squares. Chain stitching will speed up the sewing process.

6 Remove the pattern, then trim the outer edge with pinking shears leaving a fat ⅛" seam allowance. Should there be a slight puckering along the edge once it is turned, the seam allowance may be too wide and will require a bit more trimming.

7 From the right side press the seam allowance along the curved seam lines to one side with a fingernail or wooden iron. You will be amazed at how easy it is to achieve a crisp turned edge.

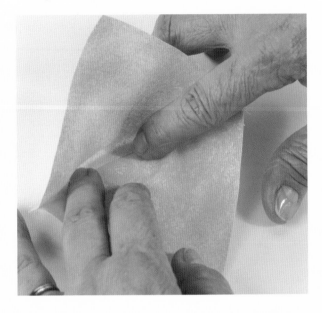

TIP

Fabric warmed with an iron will absorb water more easily than cool fabric.

8 Turn right side out, align raw edges, and press. Now spritz with a fine mist spray bottle—but go easy, getting things too wet can cause the seam allowance to pop out and not stay put. Press the fabric dry, and gently tug at the seam to separate. If the water-soluble thread does not easily release, spritz, press dry, and try again. It may be helpful if the water-soluble thread side is up when you begin.

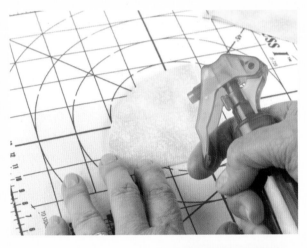

9 Lay the separated arcs seam side up. Carefully remove the regular thread, holding the seam allowance in place with your finger tips as you gently pull the thread out. Press.

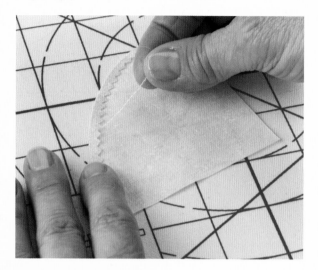

10 During construction and pressing, the straight edges of the arc segments can become irregular and may require trimming. Align a small square ruler as shown, removing any irregularities along the two straight edges.

TIP

Squaring segments, units or blocks as you construct your project is as important as pressing your project as it progresses.

11 Position the completed arc, aligning its straight edges with the corner of a base fabric square or rectangle (according to block layout in selected pattern). Meet the wrong side of the arc to the right side of the base-fabric square or rectangle and pin in place with the pins pointing toward the curve of the arc.

TIP

Instead of using pins, you can adhere the layers together using fabric glue with a fine-tip applicator that allows a very tiny drop of glue to be applied under the arc appliqué edge. The glue holds very well, takes about ten minutes to dry, and is water-soluble.

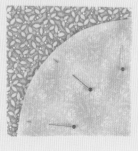

- Test your thread and stitch choices on scraps of both appliqué and base fabric. Strive for a stitch length of 2 mm or 3 mm (or 8–10 stitches per inch) and a needle position of 1.0 mm (swing of the needle into the fabric). The shorter the swing the less noticeable these stitches will be.

- Once you feel comfortable stitching in the ditch to attach the appliqué, try matching the thread to the arc fabric. I have found that a finer 50-wt. cotton thread hides the stitches better. For finer threads, select a finer 60/8 or 70/10 size needle as well.

- If your machine does not have a pin or blanket stitch, use a narrow zigzag stitch. In this case, match the thread to the appliqué or use monofilament thread. A blind hemstitch can provide an anchoring stitch, but creates a "V" shaped stitch that may not be attractive. A straight stitch is not a good choice because it is very difficult to stitch an even line of stitches along straight or curved edges. I cannot stress enough the need to test your stitch and thread choices.

- Arcs can be constructed and appliquéd by hand, which makes the stitches invisible. Glue baste the layers together or place pins on the backside to avoid catching the thread on the pins while hand stitching.

12 To stitch the arc in place, use a pin stitch. A pin stitch resembles a hand-stitched blanket stitch and is available on many new sewing machines. Matching thread to the base fabric hides any little wobbles as you learn to stitch in the ditch to sew the appliqué to the base fabric.

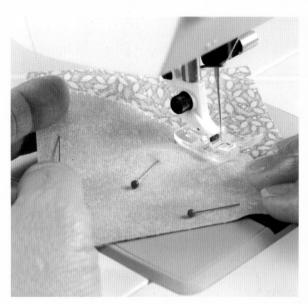

13 Turn the completed piece over so the back-side is up. Using either pinking shears or appliqué scissors, carefully trim away the excess base fabric along the curved edge of the arcs being careful not to catch the arc as you trim.

TIP

I have found a use for the trimmed-out base fabric. I once made a scrappy quilt called Dutch Treat. For this quilt, I carefully trimmed out oodles of waste arcs. I took the size of arc template that would fit the waste trim-outs and re-stitched into new arcs. I made another quilt called Dutch Treat II. From the waste trim-outs I then re-stitched and made Waste Not. I had gone around the block with those scraps for the last time and surrendered them to the circular file.

14 Place a ruler on the arc unit, aligning the unfinished size markings on the ruler with the arc unit. Trim any unevenness outside the rulers' outer edges.

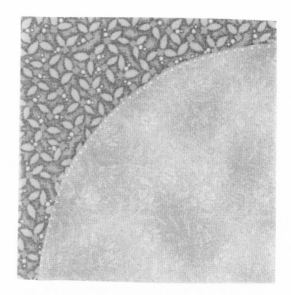

Finished and trimmed arc unit.

Baby Bow Ties

Pieced and quilted by the author

Finished size: 44" x 60" • Block size: 10½" unfinished

Seam allowance: ¼"

This quilt stitches up quick and easy, to brighten the life of that special little one in your life. Choose pastel or bright and cheery fabrics for your special creation.

Materials

All calculations based on 42" fabric width.

- 2¾ yd. for background, binding, and border
- ¾ yd. blue for border
- ¾ yd. pink
- Backing, 48" x 64"
- Batting, 46" x 62"
- Templates D and E on page 124

Cutting Instructions

Note: *For ease during construction, press all fabrics well with spray sizing prior to cutting strips.*

- **Background**

  11 strips 4½" x 42"; cut into 96 squares 4½" x 4½" for blocks

  6 strips 2¾" x 42"; cut into 88 squares 2¾" x 2¾" for inner border

  6 strips 2½" x 42" for border

  6 strips 2½" x 42" for binding

- **Blue**

  3 strips 3¼" x 42"; cut into 30 squares 3¼" x 3¼" for blocks

  3 strips 4½" x 42"; cut into 22 squares 4½" x 4½" for inner border

- **Pink**

  3 strips 3¼" x 42"; cut into 30 squares 3¼" x 3¼" for blocks

  3 strips 4½" x 42"; cut into 22 squares 4½" x 4½" for inner border

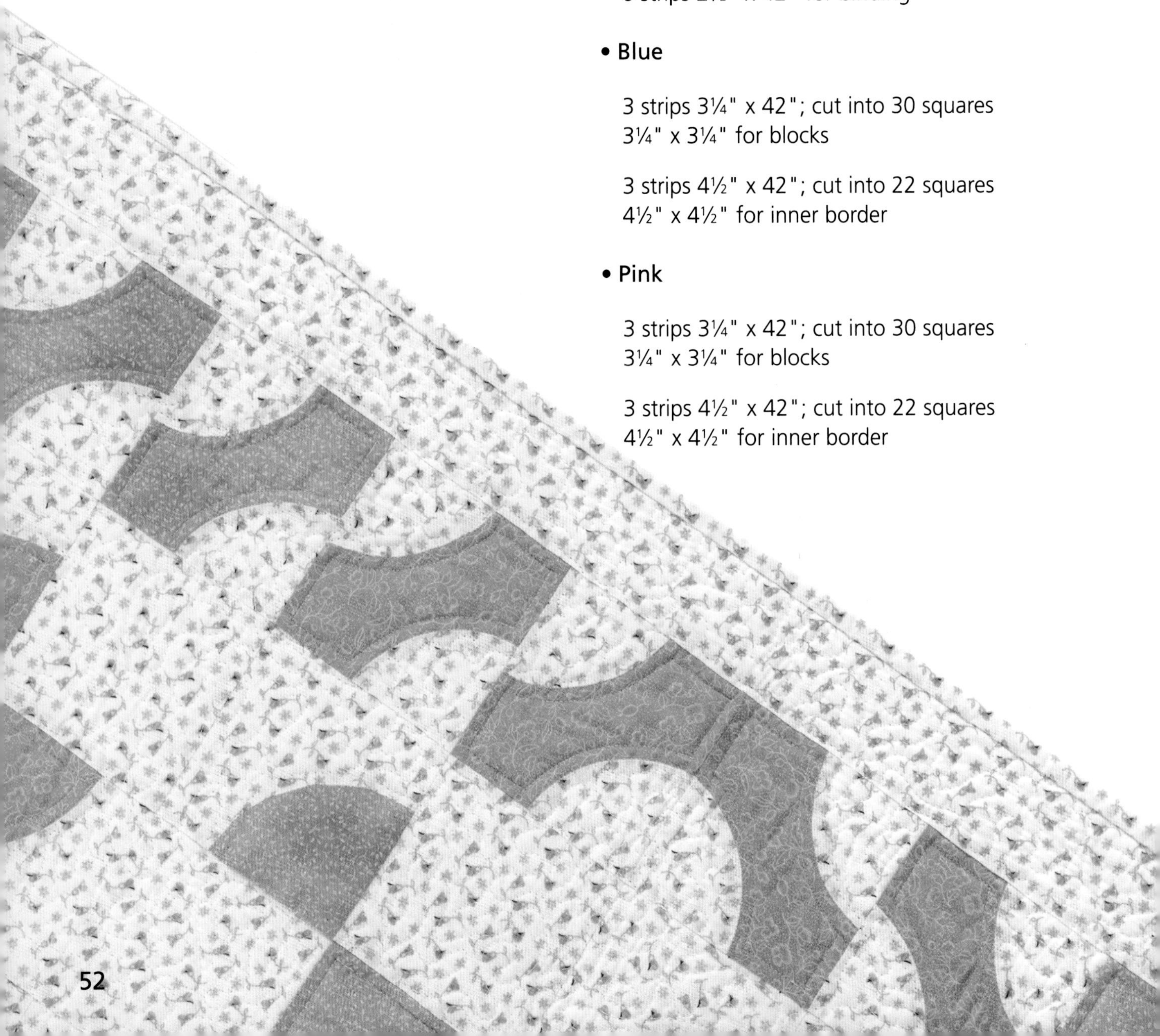

Making the Arcs

1 Trace Templates D and E from page 124. It may be helpful to trace four to six of each template for ease of sewing.

2 Place two blue 3¼" squares together with right sides facing. Pin Template D to the squares. Stitch with water-soluble thread, trim, and separate referring to Basic Arc Instructions on page 44. If necessary, trim separated arcs to 3". Make thirty arcs.

TIP

To help eliminate distortion when stitching, I try to align grain lines of the two squares.

3 Repeat step two with the pink 3¼" squares. Make thirty.

Blue 3" arc. Make 30.

Pink 3" arc. Make 30.

4 Repeat step two with Template E and background 2¾" squares. Trim arcs to 2½" as needed. Make eighty-eight.

Background 2½" arc. Make 88.

Appliqué Instructions

1 Place two background 2¼" arcs on opposite corners of a blue 4½" square. Pin in place. Appliqué by machine using a new 70/10 universal needle and a pin stitch or other decorative stitch.

2 Trim excess fabric from behind arc, taking care not to catch arc fabric with shears. Press finished blocks, and trim to 4½" x 4½" as necessary.

3 Repeat steps one and two, appliquéing forty-four background arcs to twenty-two blue 4½" squares. Appliqué the other forty-four background arcs to twenty-two pink 4½" squares.

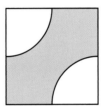 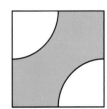

4 Place a blue arc on a background 4½" square, positioning the arc on one corner. Pin and stitch in place. Make thirty blocks and trim as necessary. Next, sew a pink D arc to a background 4½" square. Make thirty blocks and trim as necessary.

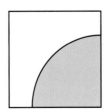 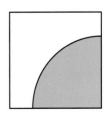

Quilt Assembly

1 Arrange block units according to the quilt diagram. Sew blocks in vertical rows. Press each block row seams in opposite directions, so each rows seams will interlock with the next. Sew vertical rows together and press these seams the same direction.

Border Assembly

1 Review Straight Borders on page 10. Measure the squared quilt top lengthwise in two or three places. Write the numbers down and average the measurements.

2 Sew two 2½" x 42" strips together for each side border. Cut to the length measurement.

3 Find the center of each side of the quilt and the center of each side border strip and mark with pins or a marking pencil. Align the centers of the strips with the quilt centers. Match the ends with the ends of the quilt and ease in any fullness. Pin and sew in place. Press seams toward the outer borders.

4 Measure the quilt top (with the attached side borders) widthwise in two or three places. Write the numbers down and average the measurements. Sew one and a half 2½" x 42" strips together for each top and bottom border. Cut to the width measurement. Repeat step three, this time attaching the top and bottom borders.

5 Press the completed top and clip any loose threads from the back.

Finishing

1 Layer your quilt top with batting and backing. Pin or hand baste the layers together.

2 Follow the quilting design shown in the diagram or quilt as desired. Bind the edges and be sure to label your quilt.

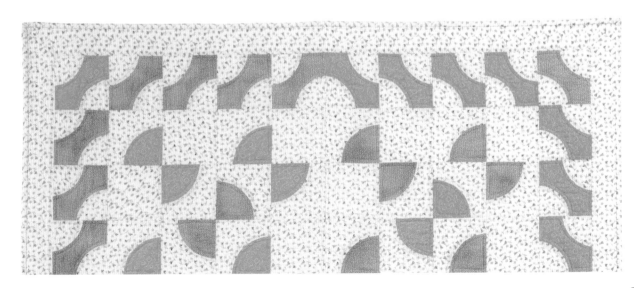

Jack's Out of the Box

Pieced by the author; quilted by Debbie Short

Finished size: 48" x 60" • Block size: 12½" unfinished

Seam allowance: ¼"

One day while doodling, I swapped arcs for the straight lines of the half-square triangles in the Jack-in-the-Box block and came up with this fun variation I call Jack's Out of the Box. I prefer two colors for this quilt, so give your favorite two-color combination a try.

Materials

All calculations based on 42" fabric width.

- 2½ yd. light blue for blocks, binding, and borders
- 5½ yd. dark blue for blocks, binding, and borders
- Backing 54" x 66"
- Batting 52" x 64" rectangle
- Template A

Cutting Instructions

Note: *Be sure to press all fabrics well with spray sizing before cutting the strips.*

- **Light Blue**

  2 strips 6½" x 42"; cut into 24 rectangles 6½" x 3½"

  8 strips 3½" x 42"; cut into 96 squares 3½" x 3½"

  3 strips 2½" x 42" for inner border

  3 strips 1½" x 42" for middle border

  4 strips 3½" x 42" for outer border

  3 strips 2½" x 42" for binding

- **Dark Blue**

  2 strips 6½" x 42"; cut into 24 rectangles 6½" x 3½"

  8 strips 3½" x 42"; cut into 96 squares 3½" x 3½"

  3 strips 2½" x 42" for inner border

  3 strips 1½" x 42" for middle border

  4 strips 3½" x 42" for outer border

  3 strips 2½" x 42" for side binding

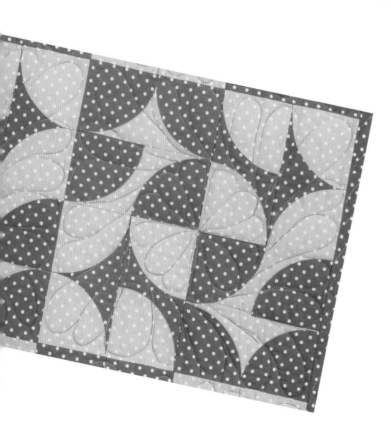

Making Block Segments

1 Trace four to six Template A pieces onto tracing paper. Template A is found on page 124.

2 Place two light-blue 3½" squares together with right sides facing. Pin Template A to the squares. Stitch around the templates with water-soluble thread. Trim and separate, referring to steps five through ten of the Basic Arc Instructions on pages 46-48. If necessary, trim separated arcs to 3¼". Make a total of ninety-six light blue arcs.

> **TIP**
>
> *Fabric warmed by an iron absorbs water faster than cool fabric.*

3 Repeat step two with the dark blue 3½" squares. Make a total of ninety-six dark blue arcs.

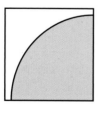

Appliqué Instructions

Unit 1

1 Place two light blue arcs on a 3½" x 6½" dark blue rectangle. Position arcs as shown. Pin or glue baste in place. Appliqué by machine using a 70/10 universal machine needle and a pin stitch or other decorative stitch.

2 After stitching, trim excess fabric from behind arc, being careful not to catch arc fabric while trimming. Press finished unit and trim to 3½" x 6½", if needed.

3 Repeat steps one and two, appliquéing a total of forty-eight light blue arcs to twenty-four dark blue 3½" x 6½" rectangles. Then, appliqué forty-eight dark blue arcs to twenty-four light blue 3½" x 6½" rectangles.

Unit 2

1 Place two light blue arcs on a dark blue 3½" x 6½" rectangle. Position the arcs as illustrated. Pin and stitch in place. Repeat, sewing a total of forty-eight light blue arcs to twenty-four dark blue 3½" x 6½" rectangles.

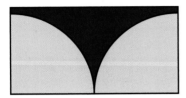

2 Place two dark blue arcs on a light blue 3½" x 6½" rectangle. Position the arcs as illustrated. Pin and stitch in place. Repeat, sewing a total of forty-eight dark blue arcs to twenty-four light blue 3½" x 6½" rectangles.

Block Assembly

1 Sew block units together following the block layout diagram. Press seams as illustrated. Square blocks to 12½".

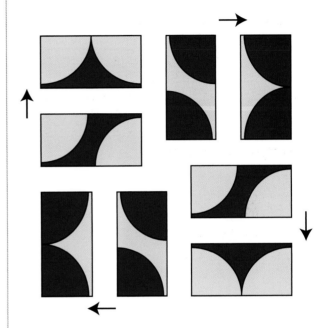

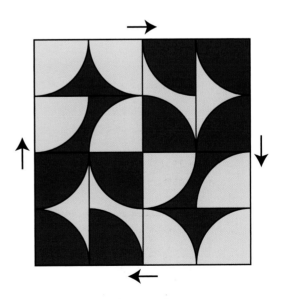

Quilt-Top Assembly

1 Assemble and sew the blocks according to the lay out diagram. Sew the blocks in vertical rows. Press the seams of each block in the row in the opposite direction of the one next to it, so the seams interlock. Sew vertical rows, and press seams the same direction.

2 Before adding the borders, square the top by working your way around the outer edge of the quilt. Align a ruler with the same block segment or unit and trim any irregularities outside the rulers' edge.

Border Assembly

The border sections for Jack's Out of The Box are built as three-piece strip sets that are constructed in opposite color ways.

1 For the top and right side sections, join one and a half 42" x 2½" dark blue strips. (Use a diagonal seam to join all border strips). Make two. Then join one and a half 42" x 1½" light blue strips. Make two. Then join two 42" x 3½" dark blue strips. Make two. Trim seam allowances to ¼" and press seams open.

2 Fold the strips in half to find the centers. Align the centers of the strips to arrange the border strips. Join a 3½" dark blue strip and a 2½" dark blue strip to either side of a 1½" light blue strip. Press seams toward the outer border. Make two.

3 For the bottom and left side border sections, join one and a half 42" x 2½" light blue strips. Make two. Then join one and a half 42" x 1½" dark blue strips. Make two. Then join two 42" x 3½" light blue strips. Make two. Trim seam allowances to ¼" and press seams open.

4 Fold the strips in half to find the centers. Align the centers of the strips to arrange the border strips. Join a 3½" light blue strip and a 2½" light blue strip to either side of a 1½" dark blue strip. Press seams toward the outer border. Make two.

5 Apply the side borders first, then the top and bottom borders. Start and stop stitching ¼" from each corner. Press seams away from the quilt. Follow the Mitered Border Instructions on page 11. Press the completed top and clip any loose threads from the back.

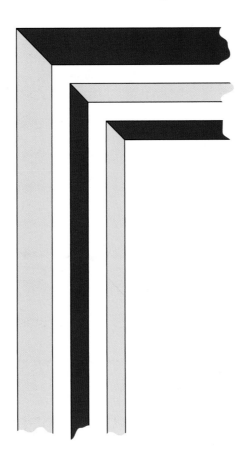

Finishing

1 Layer the quilt top with batting and backing and baste together.

2 Use the quilting motif shown in the diagram or quilt as desired.

3 Before adding the binding, it is helpful to square the top. Work your way around the outer edge of the quilt, aligning a ruler with the same block segment or unit. Trim any irregularities outside the rulers' edge.

Binding

The binding for Jack's Out of the Box is a bit different since the borders are constructed in opposite color ways.

1 Use a diagonal seam to join three light blue strips. Then join three dark blue strips. Press the binding in half so the wrong sides are together.

2 Start stitching the dark blue binding to the light blue border at the quilt's front side at the bottom right edge (the dark blue binding is sewn to the light blue border). Use a ¼" seam allowance. See step six of Binding Instructions on page 19. Apply dark blue binding to bottom and left edges only.

3 Turn the dark blue binding to the backside and hand stitch in place. Trim the ends of the dark blue binding even with the quilt edge.

4 Allowing a ½" tail, start stitching the light blue binding in place a couple stitches from the top left edge (the light blue binding is sewn to the dark blue border). Backstitch and pivot at the corner as before. Continue stitching along the right side of the quilt top. Stop stitching a couple stitches from the bottom end and backstitch.

5 Trim the ends, leaving a ½" tail. Fold the tail to the underside, then turn the binding to the backside and hand stitch in place. Take a few stitches to anchor the folded edge.

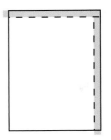

TIP

Now would be a good time to insert the quilt label under the binding at the lower left corner of the quilt back.

Liberty Twist

Pieced by the author; quilted by Johanne Moore
Finished size: 54" x 54" • Block size: 10½" unfinished
Seam allowance: ¼"

Liberty Twist is dedicated to our service men and women stationed all over the world. It's a striking quilt in red, white, and blue— however, it would look amazing in any color palette.

Materials

All calculations based on 42" fabric width.

- White 1½ yd.
- Red 1 yd. for blocks and border
- Blue 2¼ yd. for blocks, binding, and border
- Backing 3⅓ yd. (60" x 60" square)
- Batting 57" x 57" square
- Template C

Cutting Instructions

Note: For ease during construction, press all fabrics well with spray sizing prior to cutting strips.

• White

13 Strips 2½" x 42"; cut into 208 squares, 2½" x 2½"

4 Strips 4½" x 42"; cut into 64 rectangles, 4½" x 2½"

• Red

5 Strips 2½" x 42"; cut into 96 squares, 2½" x 2½"

1 Strips 4½" x 42"; cut into 16 rectangles, 4½" x 2½"

5 Strips 1½" x 42" for 2nd border; cut one strip into 4 equal pieces

• Blue

6 Strips 2½" x 42"; cut into 96 squares, 2½" x 2½"

1 Strips 4½" x 42"; cut into 16 rectangles, 4½" x 2½"

5 Strips 2½" x 42" for 1st border; cut one strip into 4 equal pieces

6 Strips 4½" x 42" for 3rd border; cut two strips in half

6 Strips 2½" x 42" wide for binding

Backing, 60" x 60" rectangle

Batting, 57" x 57" rectangle

Making Block Units

1 Trace Template C from page 124. It may be helpful to trace four to six templates for faster sewing.

2 Place two white 2½" squares together with right sides facing. Pin Template C to the squares and stitch around the template with water-soluble thread. Trim and separate, referring to steps five through ten of Basic Arc Instructions on pages 46-48. Trim separated arcs to 2¼".

3 Repeat steps one and two with 128 white 2½" squares, creating 128 white arcs. Then repeat with thirty-two red 2½" squares, creating thirty-two red arcs. Then repeat with sixteen blue 2½" squares, creating sixteen blue arcs.

White 2¼" arc. Make 128.

Red 2¼" arc. Make 32.

Blue 2¼" arc. Make 16.

Appliqué Instructions

1 Appliqué by machine using a 70/10 universal needle and a pin stitch or other decorative stitch.

2 Place one white arc on the corner of a red 2½" square. Pin in place and sew. Trim the excess fabric from behind the arc, being careful not to catch the arc fabric while trimming. Press the finished unit and trim to 2½" x 2½" square, as needed. Make forty eight.

3 Repeat steps one and two, this time appliquéing sixty-four white arcs to sixty-four blue 2½" squares. Then appliqué thirty-two red arcs to thirty-two white 2½" squares. Then appliqué sixteen blue arcs to sixteen white 2½" squares

White arc on red square. Make 48.

White arc on blue square. Make 64.

Red arc on white square. Make 32.

Blue arc on white square. Make 16.

4 Place a white arc on a red 2½" x 4½" rectangle, positioning the arc on one corner as shown. Pin and stitch in place. Make sixteen. Repeat, appliquéing a white arc to a blue 2½" x 4½" rectangle. Make sixteen.

White arc on red rectangle. Make 16.

White arc on blue rectangle. Make 16.

Block Assembly

1 Arrange and sew the units together as indicated. Then add the bottom row according to the block layout diagram. Press the seams as indicated, and trim the finished block to 10½" x 10½".

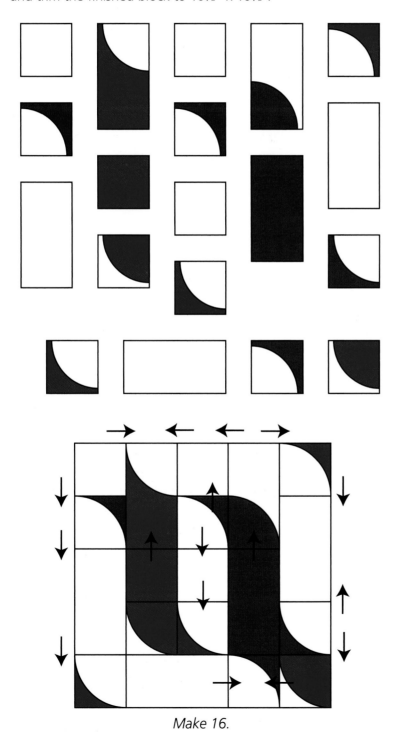

Make 16.

Quilt-Top Assembly

1 Assemble the blocks according to the quilt layout diagram. Then sew the blocks in vertical rows. Press each seams of each row's blocks in opposite directions, so the seams of each row will interlock with the next row. Stitch block rows, press seam allowances to one side.

2 Before adding the borders, it is a good idea to square the top. Work your way around the outer edge of the quilt, aligning a ruler with the same block segment or unit. With a rotary cutter, trim any irregularities outside the rulers' edge.

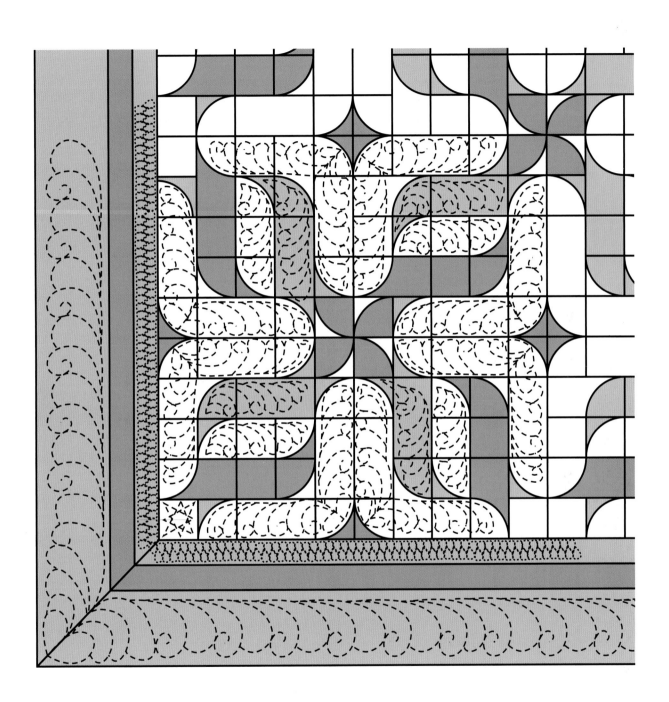

Border Assembly

1 For the blue inner border; sew one and a fourth 2½" x 42" strips together with a diagonal seam (use a diagonal seam with a ¼" seam allowance to join all strips). 42" + 10½" = 52½" each. Make four (one 52½" strip for each side). Press seams open.

2 For the red middle border; sew one and one fourth 1½" x 42" strips together. Make four (one 52½" strip for each side). Press seams open.

3 For the blue outer border; sew one and a half 4½" x 42" wide strips together. 42" + 21" = 63" each. Make four (one 63" strip for each side). Press seams open.

4 Fold the strips in half to find and mark the centers. Mark with pins or a marking pencil. To make the three-piece strip sets, attach a 4½" blue strip and a 2½" blue strip to either side of a 1½" red strip. Use the center marks to align the centers. Pin the strips together and sew. Make four (one for each side.)

5 Apply borders, referring to steps five through ten of Mitered Borders on pages 12-14. Press completed top and clip loose threads from the back.

Finishing

1 Layer the quilt top with batting and backing and pin or hand baste the layers together. Quilt according to the quilting motif shown in the diagram on page 69 or quilt as desired.

2 Assemble and apply binding. Before stitching the binding in place, lay the completed binding around the edge of the quilt, adjusting as necessary so a diagonal seam does not fall directly on a corner. Be sure to label your quilt and you're done!

Harlequin

Designed by the author, pieced and quilted by Johanne Moore
Finished size: 54" x 66" Block size: 12½" x 12½" (unfinished)
Seam allowance: ¼"

This whirly-swirly mix of color is easier to make than it looks.
When broken down into block segments the arcs are fast, fun, and easy.
The flow of this pattern lends itself to masculine colors as well as pastels.

Materials

All calculations based on 42" fabric width.

- Tan 2¼ yd.
- Rose 2¾ yd. for blocks and binding
- Brown 3 yd.
- Backing 3⅓ yd.
- Batting 58" x 70" rectangle
- Template A

Cutting Instructions

Note: *For ease during construction, press all fabrics well with spray sizing prior to cutting strips.*

- **Tan**

  20 strips, 3½" x 42"; cut into 232 squares, 3½" x 3½"

- **Rose**

  14 strips, 3½" x 42"; cut into 160 squares, 3½" x 3½"

  4 strips, 6½" x 42"; cut into 20 squares, 6½" x 6½"

  6 strips, 2½" x 42" for binding

- **Brown**

  27 strips, 3½" x 42"; cut into 316 squares, 3½" x 3½"

  Cut into 76 squares, 3½" x 3½"

  Backing, 60" x 72"

  Batting, 58" x 70"

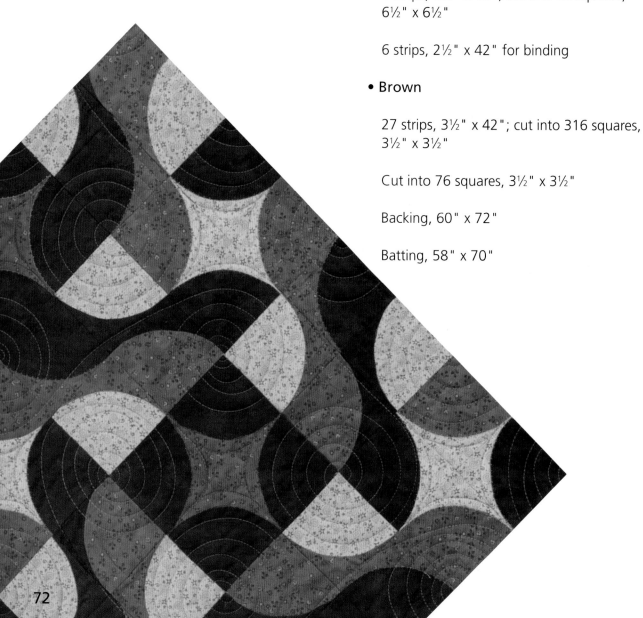

Making Block Segments

1 Trace Template A from page 124 onto freezer paper. It is helpful to make four to six templates for ease of sewing.

2 Place two tan 3½" squares with right sides facing. Pin Template A to the squares and stitch around the template with water-soluble thread. Trim around the arcs and separate, referring to step five of Basic Arc Instructions on page 46. If necessary, trim separated arcs to 3¼". Make 116 arcs.

TIP

Fabric warmed by an iron absorbs water faster than cool fabric.

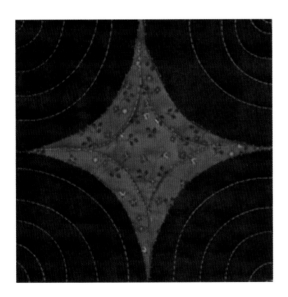

3 Repeat above with rose and brown 3½" squares. Make eighty rose arcs and 196 brown arcs.

Tan 3¼" arc. Make 116.

Rose 3¼" arc. Make 80.

Brown 3¼" arc. Make 196.

73

Appliqué Instructions

1 Stitch tan arcs to brown 3½" squares. Make seventy-six. Stitch a rose arc to a brown 3½" square. Make forty. Stitch a rose arc to a tan 3½" square. Make forty. Stitch a tan arc to a rose 3½" square. Make forty. Stitch a brown arc to a tan 3½" square. Make seventy-six. Stitch a brown arc to a rose 3½" square. Make forty. Stitch four brown arcs to a rose 6½" square. Make twenty.

Tan arc on brown square. Make 76.

Brown arc on tan square. Make 76.

Rose arc on brown square. Make 40.

Brown arc on rose square. Make 40.

Rose arc on tan square. Make 40.

Tan arc on rose square. Make 40.

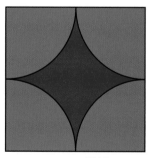

Four brown arcs on rose 6½" square. Make 20.

2 After stitching, trim excess fabric from behind each arc an ⅛" away from the stitching line. Be careful not to catch the arc fabric while trimming. Press finished segments, trim to 3½" x 3½" if needed. (Do not trim the 6½" square.)

Block Assembly

1 For Block 1, arrange and sew segments together following the block layout diagram. Press seams as illustrated. Make ten. Square blocks to 12½".

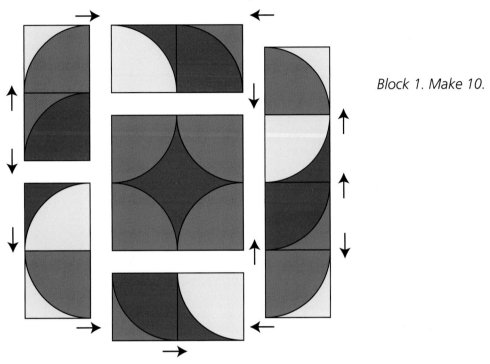

Block 1. Make 10.

2 For Block 2, arrange and sew segments together following the block layout diagram. Press seams as illustrated. Make ten. Square blocks to 12½".

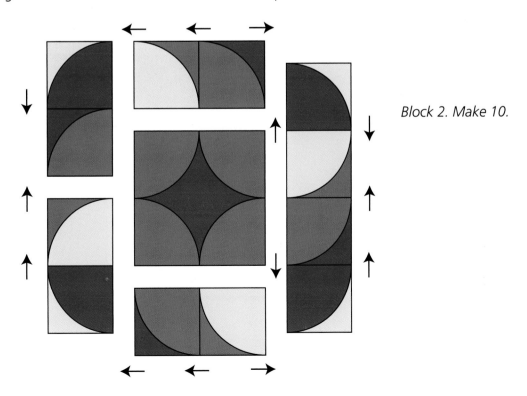

Block 2. Make 10.

Pieced-Border Assembly

1 Stitch the pieced border units together as shown. Sew ten two-piece units for each side border and eight two-piece units for each top and bottom border section. Take note that the two-piece units are oriented differently.

2 Assemble the border strips, pressing as illustrated.

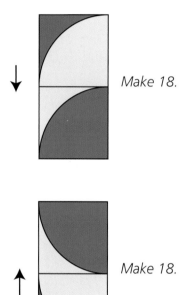

Make 18.

Make 18.

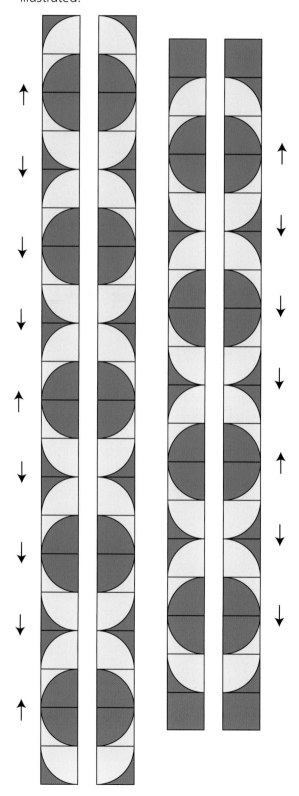

Quilt-Top Assembly

1 Lay out blocks according to the quilt diagram, stitch the blocks and border sections in vertical rows. Press the seams each row's blocks in opposite directions, so each row's seams interlock with the next. Stitch block rows together, and press seam allowances to one side.

2 Press the completed top and clip any loose threads on the back.

Finishing

1 Layer the quilt top with batting and backing. Pin or hand baste the layers together.

2 Follow the quilting motif shown in the diagram or quilt as desired.

3 Assemble and stitch the binding. Use diagonal seams to sew the six rose 2½" x 42" binding strips together. Don't forget to label your quilt.

Northern Lights

Pieced by the author; quilted by Lyn Bunyard
Finished size: 72" x 96" • Block size: 12½" unfinished
Seam allowance: ¼"

Northern Lights may look complicated, but it is super simple.
The one-block design, two sizes of arcs, and two alternating
fabric colors make it simple and quick.

Materials

All calculations based on 42" fabric width.

- 4 yd. multi-color print for blocks and binding
- 5¾ yd. black for blocks, binding, and borders
- 4½ yd. backing, 78" x 102"
- Batting 76" x 100" (black batting is preferred with black fabric)
- Templates B and C

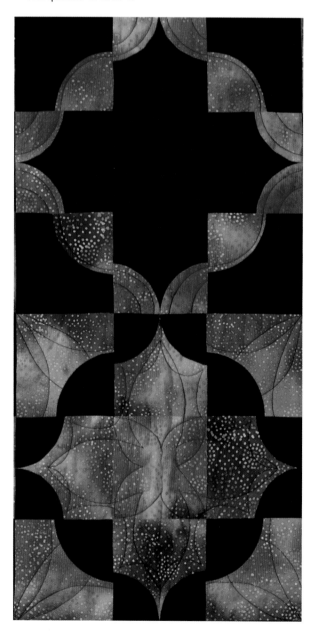

Cutting Instructions

Note: *For ease during construction, press all fabrics well with spray sizing prior to cutting strips.*

- **Black**

    17 strips, 4½" x 42"; cut into 153 squares, 4½" x 4½"

    6 strips, 3" x 42"; cut into 72 squares, 3" x 3"

    9 strips, 2½" x 42"; cut into 144 squares, 2½" x 2½"

    9 strips, 6½" x 42" for outer border

    6 strips, 8" x 42"; cut into 30 rectangles, 2½" x 8" for binding

- **Print**

    18 strips, 4½" x 42"; cut into 162 squares, 4½" x 4½"

    5 strips, 3" x 42"; cut into 68 squares, 3" x 3"

    9 strips, 2½" x 42"; cut into 136 squares, 2½" x 2½"

    6 strips, 8" x 42"; cut into 30 rectangles, 2½" x 8" for binding

    Backing, 60" x 60" rectangle

    Batting, 57" x 57" rectangle

Making the Arcs

1 Trace Templates B and C from page 124. It is helpful to make four to six of each template for faster sewing.

2 Place two black 3" squares together with right sides facing. Pin Template B to the squares. Stitch around the template with water-soluble thread, then trim and separate. Refer to steps five through ten of the Basic Arc Instructions on pages 46-48. Trim separated arcs to 2¾".

3 Repeat with remaining black 3" squares. Make seventy-two total black arcs. Then repeat with print 3" squares. Make sixty-eight print 2¾" arcs.

Black 2¾" arc.
Make 72.

Print 2¾" arc.
Make 68.

4 Repeat step two with black 2½" squares and Template C. Make 144 black 2¼" arcs. Then repeat with print 2½" squares and Template C. Make 136 print 2¼" arcs.

Black 2¼" arc.
Make 144.

Print 2¼" arc.
Make 136.

Appliqué Instructions

1 Place one black 2¾" arc on the corner of a print 4½" square. Pin in place and sew with a new 70/10 universal needle and a pin stitch or other decorative stitch. Trim excess fabric from behind arcs, taking care not to catch arc fabric with shears. Press finished blocks, and trim to 4½" x 4½" square. Make seventy two.

2 Repeat with a print 2¾" arc and a black 4½" x 4½" square. Make sixty eight.

Make 72.   *Make 68.*

3 Place two black 2¼" arcs on a print 4½" square. Position the arcs as illustrated. Pin and stitch in place. Press and trim to 4½" square as necessary. Make seventy two squares.

4 Repeat with two print 2¼" arcs on a black 4½" x 4½" square. Make 136 squares.

Make 72.

Make 136.

Block Assembly

1 There are two color ways for this block. Sew the block units together following the layout diagram for Block 1 and Block 2. Press seam allowances as indicated and square the blocks to 12½".

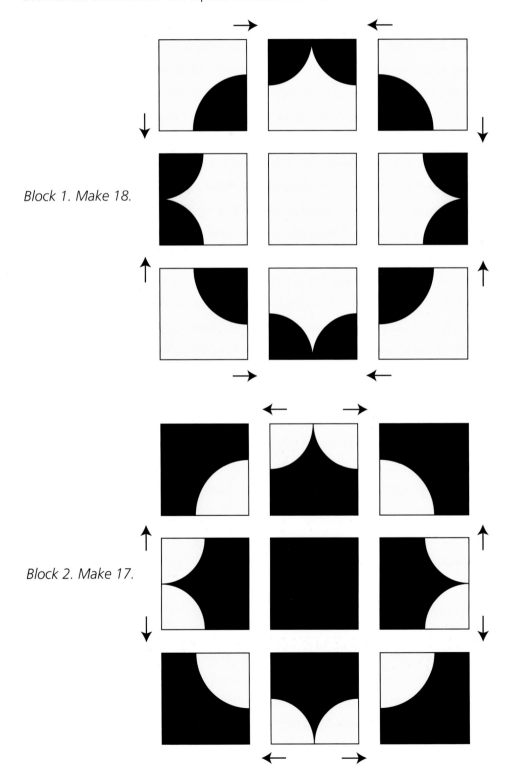

Block 1. Make 18.

Block 2. Make 17.

Quilt Top Assembly

1 Sew blocks in vertical rows. Press each row seams in opposite direction from the next row so seams interlock. Sew vertical rows, press seam the same direction.

2 Before adding the borders, it's a good idea to square the top. Work your way around the outer edge of the quilt, aligning a ruler with the same block segment and trimming any edge irregularities.

Border Assembly

1 For the black outer border, sew two 6½" x 42" strips together for each top and bottom border. Then sew two-and-a-half 6½" x 42" strips together—using a diagonal seam—for each side border.

2 Mark the centers of the borders and centers of each side of the quilt. Lining up the center marks, pin the side borders in place. If there is any ease, it can be adjusted in as you pin. Stitch the side borders to the quilt top. Then, pin and stitch the top and bottom in the same way. Press the seams toward the borders.

3 Press the completed top and clip any loose threads.

Finishing

1 Layer the quilt top with batting and backing. Pin or hand baste the layers together.

2 Use the quilting motif shown in the diagram or quilt as desired.

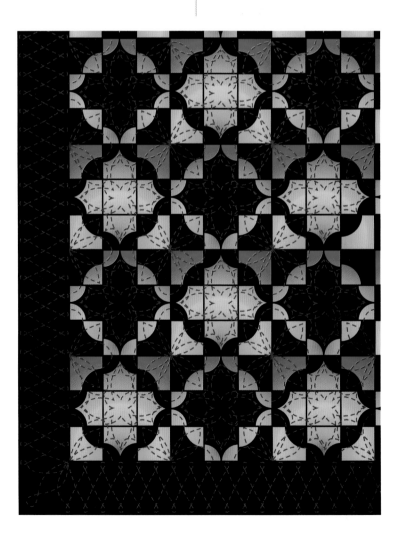

Binding

1 To assemble the binding, join alternating 2½" x 8" rectangles of black and multi-color print. Use diagonal seams. Make 345" of binding.

3 Stitch the binding to the quilt. When the ends meet, share the joining with both colors the best you can. Finish by turning the binding to the back and hand stitching in place. Be sure to label your quilt.

> **TIP**
>
> *When applying the binding, start at the lower left bottom or side. That way, the eye will not notice the joining points if they are not perfect.*

> **TIP**
>
> *For a one color binding cut nine 2½" x 42" strips and join them together with diagonal seams.*

2 Before stitching, lay the completed binding around the edge of the quilt. Adjust as necessary so a diagonal seam does not fall directly on a corner.

Spinning Stars

Pieced by Kathy Bowers, quilted by Danetta Burnett
Finished size: 62" x 86" Block size: 12½" (unfinished)
Seam allowance: ¼"

Spinning Stars is a doodle away from Hunter's Chain. Move one arc here, another there, and you end up with a fun star gazing quilt. Select three fabrics, and a galaxy of your very own is just stitches away.

Materials

All calculations based on 42" fabric width.

- 3¼ yd. background for blocks and border
- 3¾ yd. blue for blocks, binding, and border
- 1¼ yd. yellow for blocks
- 4 yd. for backing (68" x 92")
- 64" x 88" batting
- Template C

Cutting Instructions

Note: *For ease during construction, press all fabrics well with spray sizing prior to cutting strips.*

- **Background**

  6 strips 4½" x 42"; cut into 48 squares, 4½" x 4½"

  11 strips 4½" x 42"; cut into 168 rectangles, 4½" x 2½"

  8 strips 2½" x 42"; cut into 120 squares, 2½" x 2½"

  7 strips 1½" x 42" for middle border

- **Blue**

  2 strips, 4½" x 42"; cut into 24 rectangles, 4½" x 2½"

  18 strips, 2½" x 42"; cut into 288 squares, 2½" x 2½" (120 base squares and 168 squares to make arcs)

  7 strips, 2½" x 42" for 1st border

  8 strips, 4½" x 42" for 3rd border

  7 strips, 2½" x 42" for binding

- **Yellow**

  15 strips, 2½" x 42"; cut into 240 squares, 2½" x 2½" (48 base squares and 192 squares to make arcs)

Making the Arcs

1 Trace Template C from page 124. It is helpful to trace four to six templates for faster sewing.

2 Place two blue 2½" squares together with right sides facing. Pin Template C to the squares. Stitch, trim, and separate referring to steps five through ten of Basic Arc Instructions on pages 46-48. Trim separated arcs to 2¼". Make 168 blue 2¼" arcs.

TIP

Pinking the seam edge with pinking shears allows for ease along the curve once pairs are turned right side out. An extra clip or two may be necessary for some curves.

3 Repeat step two with two yellow 2½" squares. Make 192 yellow 2¼" arcs.

Blue 2¼" arc. Make 168.

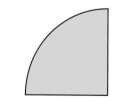

Yellow 2¼" arc. Make 192.

Appliqué Instructions

1 Position one blue 2¼" arc on the corner of a 2½" x 2½" background square. Pin and stitch in place. Trim excess fabric from behind arcs, taking care not to catch arc fabric with shears. Press finished unit, trim to 2½" x 2½" square if needed. Make ninety-six.

Blue arc to background 2½" square. Make 96.

TIP

Since there are quite a few arc segments to trim for this project, this step is a good TV project. Just be sure to trim carefully.

2 Repeat step one for each combination shown.

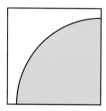

Yellow arc to background 2½" square. Make 24.

Yellow arc to blue 2½" square. Make 48.

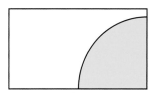

*Blue arc to background 4½" x 2½" rectangle.
Make 24.*

*Yellow arcs to background 4½" x 2½" rectangles.
Make 48.*

*Blue arc to background 4½" x 2½" rectangles.
Make 48.*

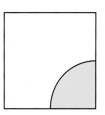

*Yellow arcs to blue 4½" x 2½" rectangles.
Make 24.*

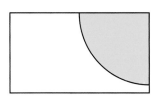

*Yellow arc to background 4½" x 2½" rectangles.
Make 24.*

*Yellow arcs to background 4½" x 4½" squares.
Make 24.*

Unit Assembly

1 Lay out and sew units together following the diagram. Press seams as directed. Press and trim completed units to 4½" square as needed.

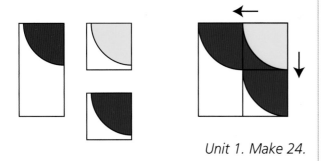

Unit 1. Make 24.

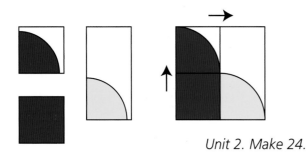

Unit 2. Make 24.

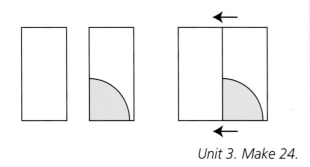

Unit 3. Make 24.

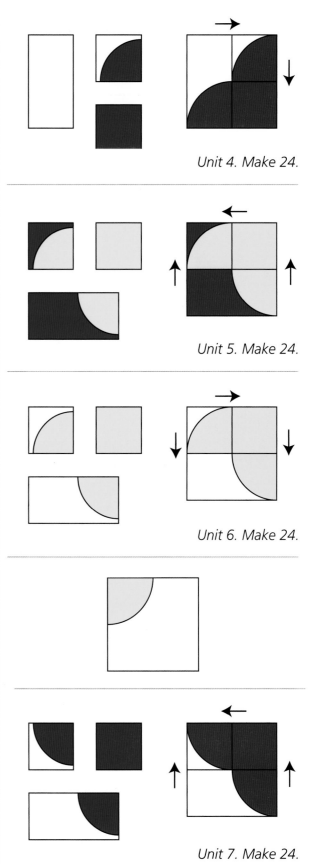

Unit 4. Make 24.

Unit 5. Make 24.

Unit 6. Make 24.

Unit 7. Make 24.

2 Assemble and sew units into blocks as diagramed. Press as shown.

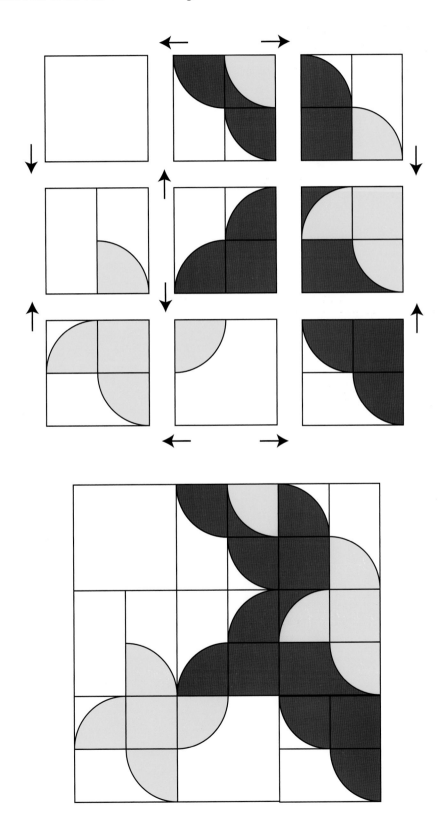

3 Here's where the hammer comes into play. I know it may be a bit unconventional, but it works well to level bulky seams. When pressing the joining seams, turn either the units or the block assembly to the back side and steam. Then whack the seam lump a couple times with the hammer. Let cool and feel the seam with your fingers. It may need a couple more whacks. Be sure your pressing surface can hold up to the hammer. For a quick alternative to the conventional ironing board; use a small block of wood with a towel on it and whack away on those unruly and bulky seams.

4 Sew blocks in vertical rows according to the block layout diagram. Press each block row seams in opposite directions so the seams interlock with the next row. Stitch the vertical rows and press the seam allowances to one side.

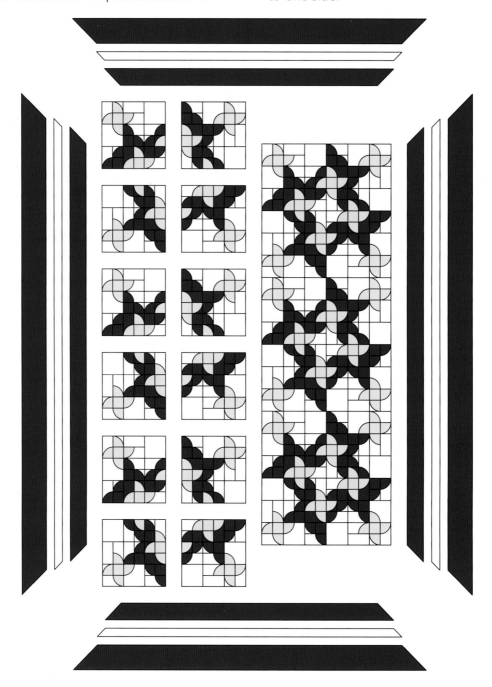

Border Assembly

1 Before adding the borders, it is a good idea to square the top. Work your way around the quilt's outer edge, aligning a ruler with the same block segment or unit and carefully trimming any edge irregularities that extend past the outer edge of the ruler.

2 For the blue inner border, sew one-and-a-half 2½" x 42" strips together. (Sew all border strips together using a diagonal seam). Make two (one for each the top and bottom border). Then sew two 2½" x 42" strips together. Make two (one for each side border).

3 For the middle border, sew one-and-a-half 1½" x 42" background strips together. Make two (one for each top and bottom border). Then sew two 1½" x 42" background strips together. Make two (one for each side border).

4 For the blue outer border, sew two full 4½" x 42" strips together. Make two (one for the top and one for the bottom). Then sew two-and-a-half 4½" x 42" strips together. Make two (one for each side).

5 Trim seam allowances to ¼" and press seams open.

6 The border strips are sewn together as three-piece units before being sewn to the quilt. To make the units, first find the centers of the strips by folding them in half and marking.

7 Sew an inner border strip and an outer border strip to either side of a middle border strip. Make four. Be sure not to mix side strips with top and bottom strips. Press seams toward the outer border.

8 Sew the three-piece units to the quilt top. Press seams toward the outer border. Press the completed top and clip any loose thread. Follow Mitered Border Instructions on page 11.

Finishing

1 Layer the quilt top with batting and backing. Pin or hand baste the layers together.

2 Use the quilting motif shown or quilt as desired.

3 Assemble and apply binding. Before stitching the binding in place, lay the completed binding around the edge of the quilt. Adjust the binding as necessary so a diagonal seam does not fall directly on a corner.

4 Be sure to label your quilt.

Hunter's Chain

Pieced by Kathy Bowers; quilted by Cora Irving
Finished size: 78" x 94" • Block size: 16½" unfinished
Seam allowance: ¼"

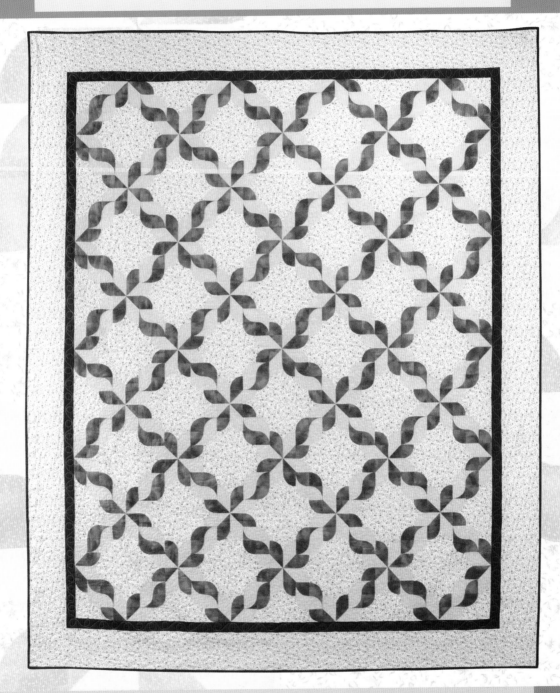

*Hunter's Chain is a spin-off doodle from the Hunter's Star pattern.
I had just made a Hunter's Star quilt and got to doodling when,
voila—Hunter's Chain was born. I hope you enjoy it as much as I do.*

Materials

All calculations based on 42" fabric width.

- 5½ yd. background for blocks and border
- 3½ yd. blue for blocks, binding, and border
- 2½ yd. yellow
- 4¾ yd. backing (84" x 100")
- 81" x 97" batting
- Template C

Cutting Instructions

Note: *For ease during construction, press all fabrics well with spray sizing prior to cutting strips.*

- **Background**

  20 strips, 2½" x 42"; cut into 320 squares, 2½" x 2½"

  19 strips, 4½" x 42"; cut into 160 squares, 4½" x 4½"

  9 strips, 6" x 42" for outer border; cut one strip in half

- **Blue**

  25 strips, 2½" x 42"; cut into 400 squares, 2½" x 2½" (80 base squares and 320 squares to make arcs)

  6 strips, 2⅞" x 42"; cut into 80 squares, 2⅞" x 2⅞"

  8 strips, 2" x 42" for inner border

  9 strips, 2½" x 42" for binding

- **Yellow**

  25 strips, 2½" x 42"; cut into 400 squares, 2½" x 2½" (80 base squares and 320 squares to make arcs)

  6 strips, 2⅞" x 42"; cut into 80 squares, 2⅞" x 2⅞"

Making the Arcs

1 Trace Template C from page 124. It is helpful to trace four to six templates for faster sewing.

2 Place two blue 2½" squares together with right sides facing. Pin Template C to the squares and stitch around the template. Trim and separate, referring to steps five through ten of Basic Arc Instructions on pages 46-48. Trim separated arcs to 2¼" as needed. Make 320.

3 Repeat step two with Template C and a yellow 2½" square. Make 320 yellow 2¼" arcs.

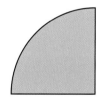

Blue 2¼" arc. Make 320.

Yellow 2¼" arc. Make 320.

Appliqué Instructions

1 Position one blue 2¼" arc on the corner of a background 2½" x 2½" square. Pin and stitch in place, referring to steps twelve through fourteen on pages 49-50. Trim excess fabric from behind arcs, taking care not to catch arc fabric with shears. Press finished unit, and trim to 2½" x 2½" as needed. Make 160.

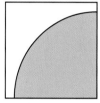

Blue arc to background 2½" square. Make 160.

> **TIP**
>
> *Since there are quite a few arc segments to trim for this project, this step is a good TV project. Be sure to trim carefully.*

2 Repeat step one for each combination shown.

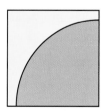

Blue arc to yellow 2½" square. Make 80.

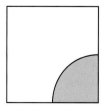

Blue arc to background 4½" square. Make 80.

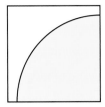

*Yellow arc to background 2½" square.
Make 160.*

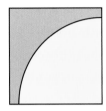

*Yellow arc to blue 2½" square.
Make 80.*

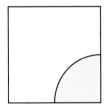

*Yellow arc to background 4½" squares.
Make 80.*

Half-Square Triangle Segment

1 Draw a diagonal line on the wrong side of a yellow 2⅞" square. With right sides together, place the yellow square on top of a blue 2⅞" square. Stitch a scant ¼" seam on both sides of the diagonal line. Make 80.

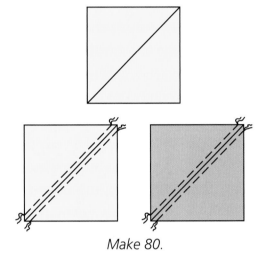

Make 80.

2 Cut along the diagonal line to yield two half-square triangle units. Press seam toward the blue fabric. Trim to 2½" if necessary. Make 160 total half-square triangle units.

Make 160.

TIP

When building blocks with a lot of pieces, you can have better accuracy if you build segments first and then construct them into units. By pressing, measuring, and trimming the units as you go, the blocks and ultimately the quilt top will be more accurate.

Unit Assembly

1 Lay out and sew the units together following the diagram. Press the seams as directed. Trim completed units to 4½" square as needed.

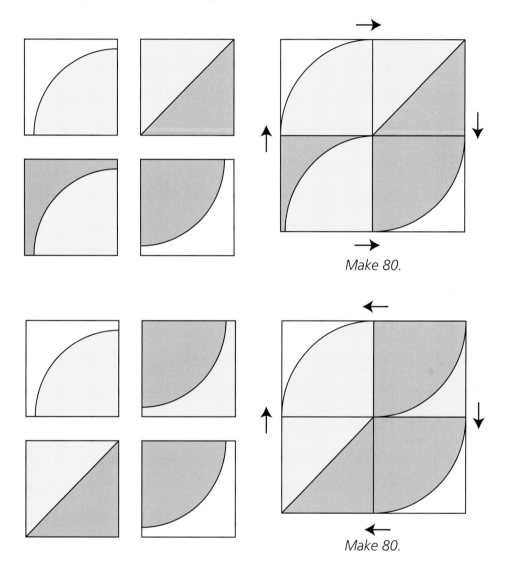

Make 80.

Make 80.

2 Here's where the hammer comes into play. I know it may be a bit unconventional, but it works well to level bulky seams. First, use your iron to press the joining seams from the front. Then turn the piece over to the back side and steam. Then whack the seam lump a couple times with the hammer. Let the piece cool and feel the seam with your fingers; it may need a couple more whacks. Be sure your pressing surface can hold up to the hammering. For a quick alternative to the conventional ironing board, place a board on a sturdy surface and wrap it with a towel. Then whack away on those unruly and bulky seams.

Block Assembly

1 Sew units into blocks according to the block layout diagram. Press as illustrated. Square blocks to 16½" x 16½".

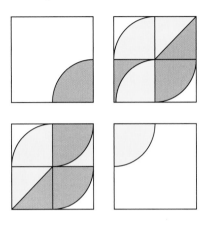

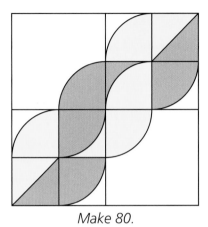

Make 80.

Make 20.

Quilt Top Assembly

1 Assemble and sew block together following the quilt layout diagram. Press seams as indicated on layout diagram. The hammer technique may be helpful at this stage of block construction as well.

2 Before adding the borders, it is a good idea to square the top. Work your way around the outer edge of the quilt, aligning a ruler with the same block segment or unit and trimming any irregularities outside the rulers' edge.

Border Assembly

1 For the inner border, stitch two blue 2" x 42" border strips together using a diagonal seam. Make four (one for each side). Measure and apply the border according to steps three and four of Straight Borders on page 10.

2 For the outer border, sew two-and-a-half background 6" x 42" strips together using a diagonal seam. Make two (one for each side). Then sew two 6" x 42" background strips together for the top and bottom outer border. Use diagonal seams. Repeat the measuring and marking process, stitch borders in place, and press seam allowances toward the border.

3 Press completed top and clip any loose threads on the back.

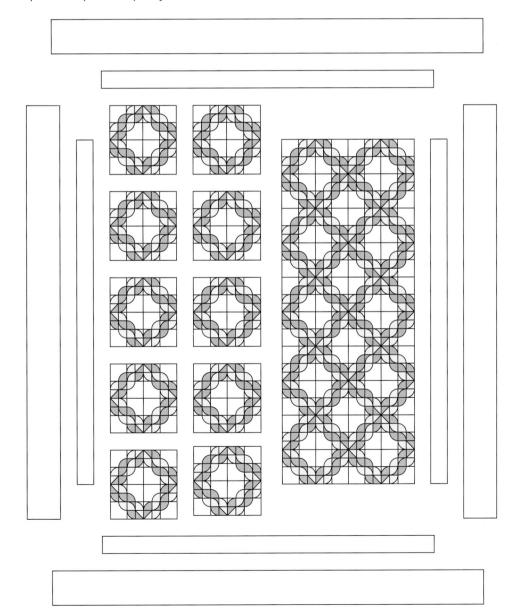

Finishing

1 Layer the quilt top with batting and backing. Pin or hand baste the layers together.

2 Use the quilting motif shown or quilt as desired.

3 Assemble the binding. Before stitching the binding in place, lay the completed binding around the edge of the quilt. Adjust as necessary so a diagonal seam does not fall directly on a corner. Apply the binding, referring to Binding instructions on page 19.

Matthew's Quilt

Pieced by the author; quilted by Debbie Short
Finished size: 46" x 58" • Block size: 6½" unfinished
Seam allowance: ¼"

*Grandson Matthew's Quilt is definitely bright and cheery in primary colors.
A bit more complex in construction, the unit placement guide makes quick
work of unit assembly.*

*When I made this quilt, all I had left were scraps. So, with a bit of creative
piecing, the outer border made for an interesting finish.*

Materials

All calculations based on 42" fabric width.

- 2 yd. blue for blocks and binding
- 1½ yd. red
- 1¾ yd. yellow
- 3 yd. backing, 52" x 64"
- 50" x 62" batting
- Template plastic
- Templates A and Unit 4 Placement Guide

Cutting Instructions

Note: *For ease during construction, press all fabrics well with spray sizing prior to cutting strips.*

- **Blue**

  8 strips 3½" x 42"; cut into 96 squares 3½" x 3½" for arcs

  5 strips 2" x 42" for 1st border; cut one strip in quarters

  1 strip 3½" x 42"; cut into 4 rectangles 3½" x 8" for outer border triangles

- **Red**

  2 strips 7⅜" x 42"; cut into 9 squares 7⅜" x 7⅜"

  2 strips 3½" x 42"; cut into 20 squares 3½" x 3½"

  1 strip 2¾" x 42"; cut into 14 squares 2¾" x 2¾"

  4 strips 3⅞" x 42"; cut into 36 squares 3⅞" x 3⅞", cut once on the diagonal (Triangle A)

  4 strips 3½" x 42" for outer border; cut into 2 rectangles 3½" x 26" and 2 rectangles 3½" x 33"

- **Yellow**

  2 strips 7⅜" x 42"; cut into 9 squares 7⅜" x 7⅜"

  1 strip 4½" x 42"; cut into 7 squares 4½" x 4½"; cut twice on the diagonal (Triangle B)

  1 strip 6½" x 42"; cut into 10 rectangles 6½" x 3½"

  3 strips 4¾" x 42"; cut into 18 squares 4¾" x 4¾"

  4 strips 3½" x 42" for outer border; cut into 2 rectangles 3½" x 26" and 2 rectangles 3½" x 33"

Making the Arcs

1 Trace Template A and the Unit 4 Placement Guide from pages 124-125. It may be helpful to trace four to six of Template A for faster sewing. The placement guide can be traced to template plastic.

2 Place two blue 3½" squares together with right sides facing. Pin Template A to the squares. Stitch around the templates. Trim and separate the squares, referring to steps six through ten of Basic Arc Instructions on pages 46-48. Trim separated arcs to 3¼". Make 96.

> ## TIP
> *To help eliminate distortion when stitching, I try to align grain lines of the two squares.*

Unit Construction

Unit 1

1 Place one red 7⅜" square on top of one yellow 7⅜" square with right sides together. Mark a diagonal line from corner to corner on one of the squares as illustrated. Stitch a scant ¼" on each side of the drawn line.

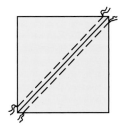

2 Press the stitching line to set the stitches, and cut the sewn unit apart on the drawn line. Open the unit, pressing the seam allowance toward the darker fabric.

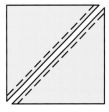 

3 On the wrong side of one open triangle unit, draw another diagonal line from corner to corner through the triangles. With the marked unit on top, match both triangle units with contrasting fabric facing and stitch on each side of the drawn line. Press to set the stitches, and then cut the units apart between the stitching lines as before.

4 To allow the seams to lay in a circular direction (to eliminate bulk at center), pick out the few stitches from the seam line of the first sewn seam. Wiggle the center of the seam, opening it to form what looks like a tiny four-patch. Press the seam in a circular fashion. From each pair of fabric squares, two 6½" quarter-triangle units are made. Make seventeen quarter-square triangle units (you will have one extra unit).

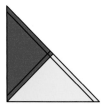 

Quarter-square triangle. Make 17.

5 Pin a blue arc on each corner of the quarter-triangle unit. Stitch the arc in place using a pin stitch or a stitch of your choice, matching the thread to the arc. Try for the shortest swing of the needle as you are comfortable with. The narrower you can go, the less the stitches will show.

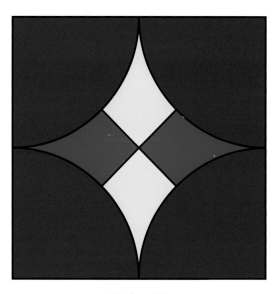

Make 17.

6 Trim the excess fabric from behind the newly stitched arcs and press. If necessary, trim the blocks to 6½" square. Refer to step eleven of the Basic Arc Instructions on page 48.

Unit 2

1 Mark a diagonal line from corner to corner on twenty red 3½" squares. Sew two red 3½" squares to each yellow 3½" x 6½" rectangle. Stitch on the line from corner to corner and trim the excess. Press the seam toward the triangles. Make ten units.

Unit 2. Make 10.

Unit 3

1 Place two red Triangle As on opposite corners of a yellow 4¾" square with right sides together and pin. Stitch in place. Fold the triangles into place and press the seams toward the triangle. Center and sew two more red Triangle As to the remaining sides of the square, press seams toward the triangle. Make eighteen units.

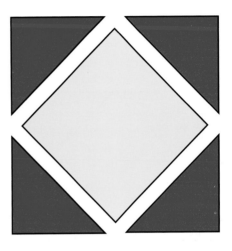

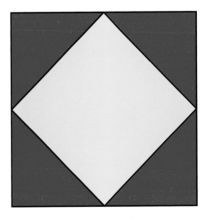

Unit 3. Make 18.

Unit 4

1 Stitch one yellow Triangle B to one edge of a red 2¾" square—take care in orienting the triangle. Press the seam toward the triangle. Stitch a second yellow Triangle B to the second side of the red square. Again note how the triangle is placed. Make fourteen base units.

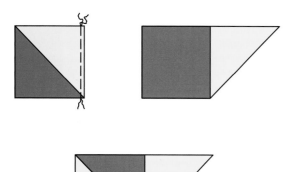

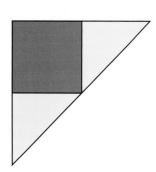

Unit 4. Make 14.

Note: *These little triangles have bias edges on the corners, so handle them carefully. The spray sizing you used to press your fabric prior to cutting will help stabilize those stretchy edges.*

2 Tape your placement guide (template found on page 126) to your work surface, so it will stay put while you work. Lay a base unit you created in step one onto the placement guide. Match the seam lines with the drawn lines on the guide.

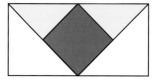

3 Place two blue arcs on the triangle base unit, matching the arc edges with the lines on the guide. Pin and stitch arcs in place.

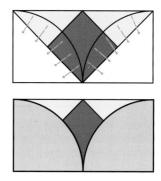

Unit 5

1 Place one red 3⅞" square on top of one yellow 3⅞" square with right sides together. Mark a diagonal line from corner to corner as illustrated. Stitch a scant ¼" on both sides of the drawn line. Cut on the drawn line. Open and press the seam toward the red fabric.

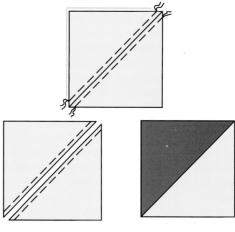

Unit 5. Make 4.

Quilt Top Assembly

1 Arrange the blocks according to the layout diagram. Stitch the blocks in vertical rows. Take care that the red points of Unit 1 are arranged properly when sewing your rows together. Also, note that the red point of Unit 4 is oriented according to the layout diagram.

2 Press the seams of each row in opposite directions of one another, so the seams will interlock with the seams in the next row. Then, stitch the rows together and press the completed top.

Border Assembly

The borders will start as individual strips. Then they will be assembled and applied as complete units.

1 For the first border, sew three blue 2" x 42" strips together. Cut this long piece in half into two pieces 2" x 60". Set aside with the remaining two blue 2" strips.

2 The outer border is a little more challenging with the insertion of the triangle; follow the next step carefully and all will go well. We'll start with the top and bottom outer border sections. Place one blue 3½" x 8" rectangle right side up on your work surface. Lay one 26" red strip on the blue rectangle with right sides facing. Mark a stitching line from corner to corner and stitch. Then trim the excess fabric and carefully press the seam away from the blue triangle.

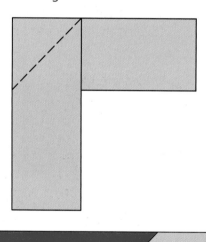

3 Measure in a ½" from the end of one yellow 3½" x 26" strip. With a ruler and a marking pencil, mark a stitching line at a 45-degree angle starting at the ½" point.

4 Now for the tricky part. Lay the yellow strip onto the blue and red strip with right sides together as shown. The ½" point should overlap the point of the red strip by ½" as shown. If you lay a ruler ¼" from the top edge of the red and blue strip, the ruler will fall on the intersection of the 45-degree line on the yellow strip and the seam of the red and blue strip. (In other words, the intersection of the 45-degree line and the red and blue seam is a ¼" below the top edge of the red and blue strip). Pin the yellow strip in place, and stitch along the marked line. Trim the excess fabric and press the seam away from the blue triangle. Repeat for remaining bottom borders.

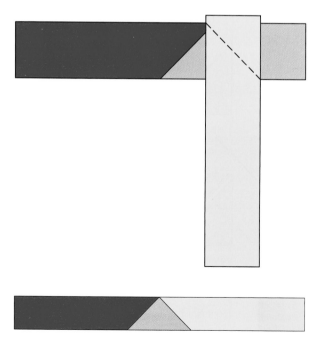

5 Repeat the above process for the side border sections using the 3½" x 33" red and yellow pieces.

6 Find the center of the blue inner border pieces and the outer border sections. Mark the centers with a pin.

7 Assemble the border units. With right sides facing, align the center of one top outer border and the center of one blue 2" x 42" inner border. Using a ¼" seam, sew these two border pieces together. Press seam toward the blue border. Repeat this process with the remaining border sections.

Applying the Borders

1 On each corner of the quilt top, mark a dot ¼" in from both edges. Match the centers of the border units with the centers of the top and bottom edges of your quilt top. Pin in place. Start stitching at the ¼" dot. Do a backstitch or two but do not go beyond the dot. Repeat with the side border units. Press seams toward the blue border. Refer to Mitered Border Instructions on page 11.

2 Press the completed top, and remove any loose threads.

Finishing

1 Layer your quilt top with batting and backing. Pin or hand baste the layers together.

2 Follow the quilting motif shown in diagram or quilt as desired. Bind the edges and be sure to label your quilt.

Basic Melon Instructions

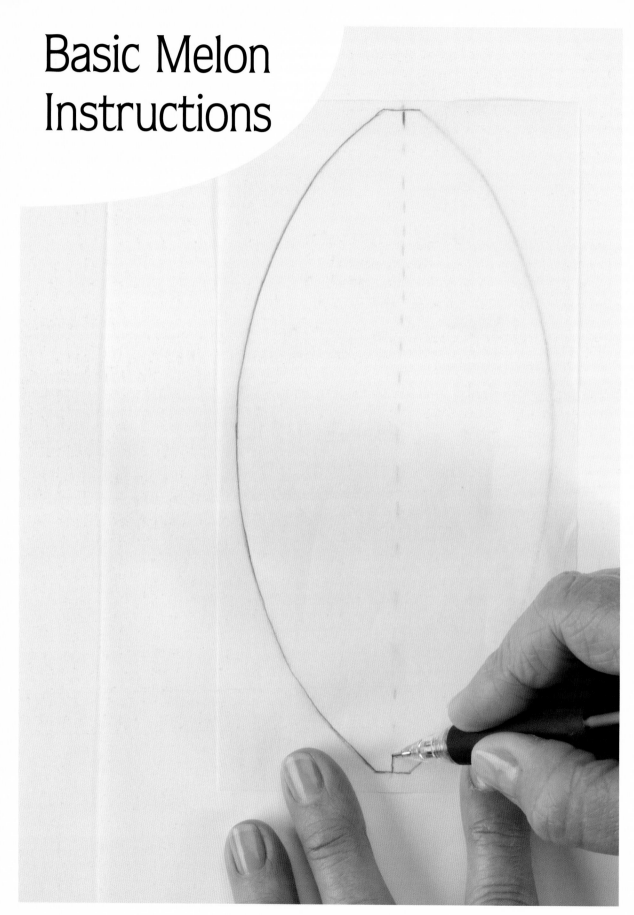

I have found that most mirror-image curved piecing can be done with water-soluble thread, including the melon shape. Moving from frames and arcs, you will find making melons easy and fun. The technique for making melons is a bit different—but, wow, do they sew up fast!

Melon Construction

1 Press frame fabric well using spray sizing prior to cutting. Spray sizing gives fabric firmness as well as a nice crisp turned-under seam edge in preparation for the appliqué process.

2 Cut fabric rectangles to desired size for project.

3 Trace the melon template from page 126 onto tracing paper. Be sure to transfer the registration marks as well.

4 To set up your machine, place water-soluble thread in the bobbin and regular thread in the top. Insert a new size 70/10 universal needle. If you experience skipped stitches, change to an 80/12 universal needle.

Should you choose to thread the water-soluble thread in the needle, lower the upper tension two or three numbers—and don't lick the thread when threading the needle!

5 Place two rectangles together with right sides facing. Pin the melon template to the rectangles, and transfer the registration marks to the fabric at each end of the template.

The pattern remains in place until stitching is complete.

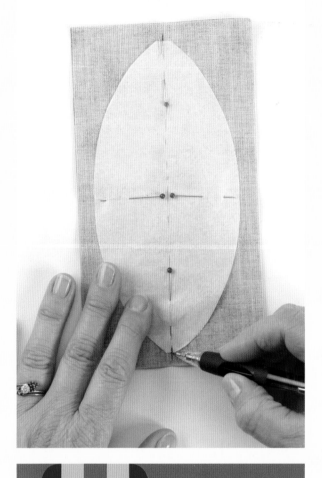

- Be sure to mark the bobbin so you don't mistake it for regular white thread.

- Remember to remove the water-soluble thread from your machine when template stitching is complete.

- Store the spool of water-soluble thread and the bobbin in a plastic bag with a silica pack to keep it moisture free.

TIP

In some sewing machines, threading the water-soluble thread in the top tension results in thread breakage. Putting it in the bobbin eliminates the problem.

TIP

Lessening the pressure on the presser foot can help you maneuver around curves.

6 Stitch around the entire outer edge of the melon template using a stitch length of 2.0 mm or 14 stitches per inch. With a short stitch length, backstitching is not usually necessary. Pin several templates to several rectangle pairs and chain stitch to speed up the sewing process.

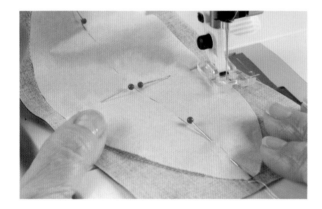

7 Remove the pattern template and trim the outer edge with pinking shears, leaving a fat ⅛" seam allowance.

8 Next, place the trimmed melon on a cutting mat. Align a ruler with the registration marks at each end of the melon. With a rotary cutter, cut down the center to separate.

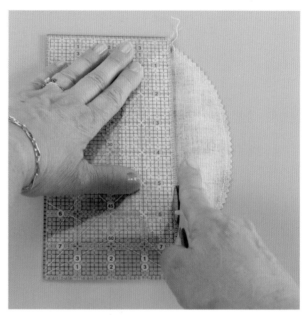

9 From the right side, press the seam allowance to one side with a fingernail or a wooden iron along the curved seam lines. You will be amazed at how easy it is to achieve a crisp turned edge. Turn the melon shapes right side out and align the raw edges. Should there be any puckering once the melon is turned right side out, a few clips along the seam allowance may be needed.

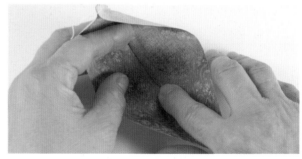

10 Since the melon shapes are long and slender, they will stretch more than frames or arcs—bias is working against us here. So, prior to pressing, we need to make a blocking cloth to help maintain the melon's length.

- A blocking cloth is a special piece of fabric marked with a line that corresponds to the block segment being constructed and pressed. Place the straight edge of your curved piece along the blocking-cloth line while pressing as an aid to keep things from stretching out of shape.

11 Select a piece of muslin or other light-colored fabric square cut 3" or 4" larger than your project. In the center of the square, draw a line the length of the finished melon. Place a hash mark at each end of the line. Stiffen the blocking cloth with a few pressings of spray sizing.

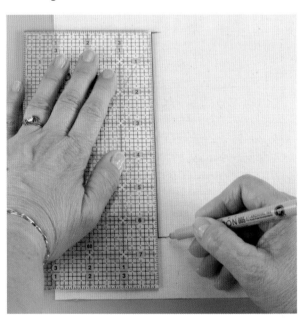

TIP

Fabric warmed with an iron will absorb water more easily than cool fabric.

12 Position a melon pair on the blocking cloth, aligning the melon on the drawn line. Place a pin in each end of the melon at the hash marks and press. Then spritz with a fine mist spray bottle, but go easy, getting things too wet can cause the seam allowance to pop out and not stay put. Press the fabric dry, and gently tug at the seam to separate. If the water-soluble thread does not easily release, spritz, press dry, and try again. It may be helpful if the water-soluble thread side is up when you begin.

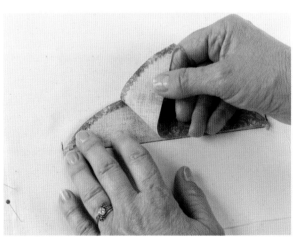

13 Lay the melons seam side up on your pressing surface. Hold the seam allowance in place with your fingers tips and gently pull the thread out. Press.

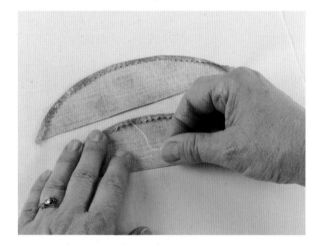

14 During construction and pressing, the straight edges of the melon segments can become irregular and may require trimming. To do this, align a small ruler as shown. Place the ½" mark on the edge at one end and the 7" mark with the edge on the other end of the melon shape. This allows the ½" mark and the 7" mark of the ruler to hang over each end of the melon, helping you to see just where the ruler needs to be to trim the melon to a finished length of 6½".

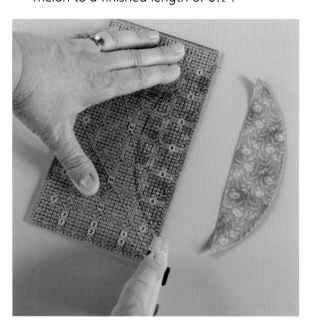

15 Position the finished melon on the base fabric rectangle. The melon ends should line up with the ends of the rectangle. Pin in place with points of the pin toward the curve of the melon. Another option is to use wash-out fabric glue with a very fine applicator tip that allows a tiny drop of glue to be applied under the edge of the melon appliqué. The glue holds very well, takes about ten minutes to dry, and is water-soluble.

16 Use a pin stitch to stitch the melon in place. The pin stitch is available on many newer sewing machines; it resembles a hand-stitched blanket stitch.

17 Turn the completed piece over so the wrong side is up. Using either pinking shears or appliqué scissors, carefully trim away the excess base fabric along the curved edge of the melons. Don't catch the melon as you trim.

18 Trim the finished melon unit to size according to the pattern requirements. Sewing, stitching, and pressing can cause edges to be irregular and a little trimming may be necessary. Please take the time to check, your finished quilt will thank you for it.

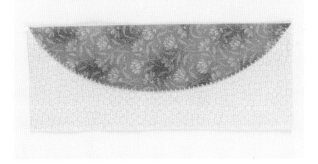

- Matching your thread to the base fabric hides any little wobbles as you learn to stitch in the ditch to sew the appliqué to the base fabric.

- Test your thread and stitch choices on scraps of both appliqué and base fabric. Strive for a stitch length of 2 mm or 3 mm and a needle position of 1.0 mm (swing of the needle into the fabric). The smaller the swing, the less noticeable these stitches will be.

- Once you feel comfortable stitching in the ditch to attach the appliqué to the base fabric, try matching the thread color to the arc fabric. I have found that a finer 50-wt. cotton thread hides the stitches well. For finer threads, select a finer size 60/8 or 70/10 needle.

- If your machine does not have a pin or blanket stitch, use a narrow zigzag stitch. In this case, match the thread to the appliqué or use monofilament thread. A blind hemstitch can provide an anchoring stitch, but creates a "V" shaped stitch that may not be attractive. A straight stitch is not a good choice, because it is very difficult to stitch an even line of stitches along straight or curved edges. I cannot stress enough the need to test your stitch and thread choices on scraps of your project fabrics.

- Lastly, the melons can be appliquéd to the base fabric by hand, making the stitches invisible. Glue baste the layers together or baste by placing the pins on the backside, which prevents thread from catching on the pins while hand stitching.

Meloncholy

Pieced by Kathy Bowers; quilted by Danetta Burnett
Finished size: 58" x 74" • Block size: 8½" unfinished
Seam allowance: ¼"

Meloncholy is just too fun. It is a spin on the orange-peel block but much easier. Each melon pattern—when it is stitched, cut, and turned—creates four melon shapes, making enough for one block. Resize the melon for a variety of projects.

Materials

All calculations based on 42" fabric width.

- 3¼ yd. blue for blocks, binding, and first border
- 1½ yd. yellow
- 2¼ yd. print for melons
- 2½ yd. striped border print for outer border (cut on the lengthwise grain)
- 3¾ yd. backing, 64" x 80" (two pieces seamed horizontally)
- 62" x 78" batting
- Template F

Cutting Instructions

Note: *Press all fabrics well with spray sizing prior to cutting strips for ease of construction.*

- **Blue**

  6 strips 6½" x 42"; cut into 96 rectangles, 6½" x 2½"

  3 strips 4½" x 42"; cut into 24 squares, 4½" x 4½"

  6 strips 2½" x 42" for inner border

  7 strips 2½" x 42" for binding

- **Yellow**

  6 strips 6½" x 42"; cut into 96 rectangles, 2½" x 6½"

  3 strips 4½" x 42"; cut into 24 squares, 4½" x 4½"

- **Print**

  10 strips 7⅛" x 42"; cut into 96 rectangles, 3¾" x 7⅛"

- **Striped Border Print (outer border)**

  Cut or tear lengthwise, two 6½" x 80" strips and two 6½" x 62" strips

  Plan the width of the outer border according to the width of the stripes or combination of strips in the border print.

- **Piping**

  6 strips 1" x 42"; cut one strip in half

Making Segments

Creating melons is similar to making arcs but with a bit of a twist. Trace a few F templates and we will get started.

Melons require stitching completely around the template. I know you are scratching your heads, "closed stitching", how does this work? You will soon understand.

1 Trace Template F from page 126 onto tracing paper. It is helpful to trace four to six of Template A for faster sewing.

2 Place two print 3¾" x 7⅛" rectangles together with right sides facing. Center and pin a Template F melon to the two rectangles. Transfer the registration mark from template to fabric by marking a small dot or line at the end of each melon. Stitch around the template with water-soluble thread and remove template. See steps four through six on pages 113-114.

3 Trim around each melon pair with pinking shears, leaving a fat ⅛" seam allowance. Mark a line down the center of the melon. With a rotary cutter and ruler, cut down the center from end to end on the marked dot or line.

4 Press the seam to one side along the seam line on the right side of the fabric with a fingernail. Turn the melon right side out.

5 Before pressing, we need to make a blocking cloth. A blocking cloth will help keep things from distorting or stretching while pressing and separating the units. To make a blocking cloth, press an 8" x 10" piece of muslin with spray sizing so it's firm. With a ruler and pencil, mark a 6½" line on the muslin with a ½" line on each short end of the line. Refer to step eleven of Basic Melon Instructions on page 115.

6 With the melon segments turned and finger pressed, lay the cut edges together along the drawn line. Match the melon points to each end of the drawn line on the blocking cloth. Place a pin in each end of the melon, anchoring it to your pressing surface. With the edges even, press with a dry iron, spritz with water, and press dry. Remove the pins and separate the two melon pieces.

7 Repeat with the remaining ninety-four print 3¾" x 7⅛" rectangles (forty-six pairs), creating 192 melon segments. Trim the separated melons to 1⅝" x 6½".

Melon Unit Appliqué Instructions

1 Position one melon shape on a blue 2½" x 6½" rectangle. Pin and stitch in place. Trim the excess fabric from behind the arc, taking care not to catch the arc fabric with shears. Press the finished unit and trim to 2½" x 6½". Make ninety six.

2 Repeat step one, this time appliquéing a print melon to a yellow 2½" x 6½" rectangle. Make ninety six.

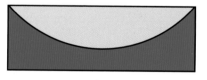

Make 96.

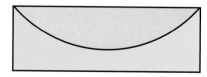

Make 96.

Block Assembly

Block 1

TIP

To assemble the blocks, you will sew the rectangle units from page 120 to 4½" x 4½" squares. To start you will sew a partial seam to begin joining the units.

1 Place a 4½" blue square right side up on your work surface. Place a yellow rectangle unit right side down, matching the long edge of the melon with the square. Align the bottom and right edges, and stitch with a scant ¼" seam. Start sewing to the half-way mark of the 4½" square. This leaves the top end of this piece unstitched. Press the seams toward the yellow rectangles, away from the blue center square.

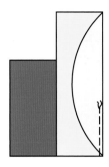

2 Turn the block a quarter turn and apply another yellow rectangle unit. Match the edges, stitch the full length of the seam, and press the seam toward the yellow rectangle.

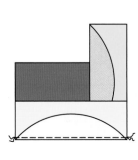 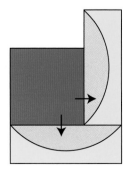

3 Add two more yellow rectangle units. To attach the fourth unit, the first unit needs to be folded out of the way. After the fourth unit has been stitched in place and the seam has been pressed, finish stitching the first unit and press. Trim to 8½" square. Create twenty-four blocks.

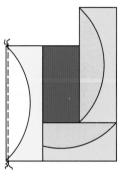

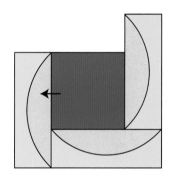

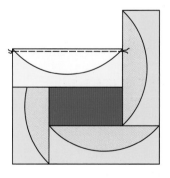

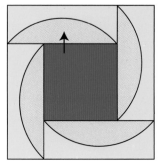

Block 1. Make 24.

Block 2

1 Repeat the steps for Block 1 with yellow base squares and blue rectangle units. The colors will spin in opposite directions. Start this block with the yellow square right side up. Place a blue base melon unit right side down. Match the long edge of the melon with the lower edge and right corner of the yellow square. Be sure to press seam toward the yellow center square. Create twenty-four blocks, and trim to 8½" square.

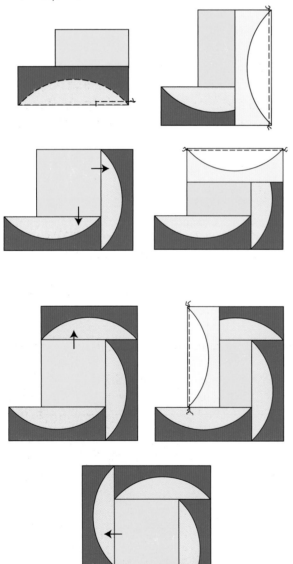

Block 2. Make 24.

Quilt Assembly

1 Follow the quilt layout diagram to assemble the blocks. Note that the block colors alternate. Press the seams of each row in opposite directions. Sew the rows together, interlocking the seams. Press these seams all in the same direction.

Border Assembly

The border assembly for Meloncholy includes a flat piping sewn to the first border. Sew the first and second borders together, and then sew to the quilt as a unit, finishing with mitered corners.

1 To assemble the flat piping, use a diagonal seam to sew one half strip to each of two 1" x 42" strips. The two resulting strips are for the top and bottom border. Next, stitch two full strips together. Make two. These are for the side borders.

2 For the inner border, join one half strip to each of two of the 2½" x 42" inner-border strips. The two resulting strips are for top and bottom border. Then sew two full strips together. Make two (one for each side border). Use diagonal seams to join all strips.

3 To add the flat piping to the inner border, find and mark the centers of the adjoining piping strips and the centers of the inner border strips. Set your machine to sew a ½" seam allowance.

4 Lay the piping piece on the appropriate inner border piece with right sides together. Match the center marks. Stitch in place along the long edge of the strip using a ½" seam allowance. The stitching line will go down the center of the piping strip. Fold and press the piping over the stitching line, meeting the raw edges. Now the piping is nice and flat and it will not twist, flip, or flare out.

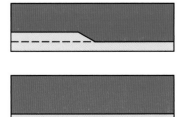

5 The outer border is from a border print. I usually tear the borders when I'm on the lengthwise grain. One word of caution, some fabrics may not be printed exactly on the grain. However, this one was and the strips were torn a little wider so the machine quilter had plenty of room to work.

TIP

Borders made from the lengthwise grain of fabric are easier to apply and hang better as well.

6 Assemble the border pieces by matching the centers and stitching along the long edges. Press the completed top, and clip any loose threads. Refer to Mitered Border Instructions on page 11.

Finishing

1 Layer your quilt top with batting and backing. Pin or hand baste the layers together.

2 Use the quilting design shown in the diagram or quilt as desired.

3 Bind the edges and be sure to label your quilt.

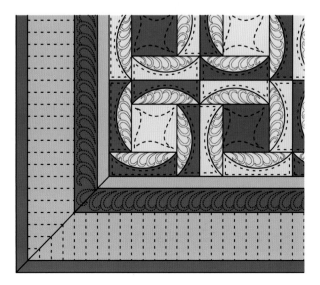

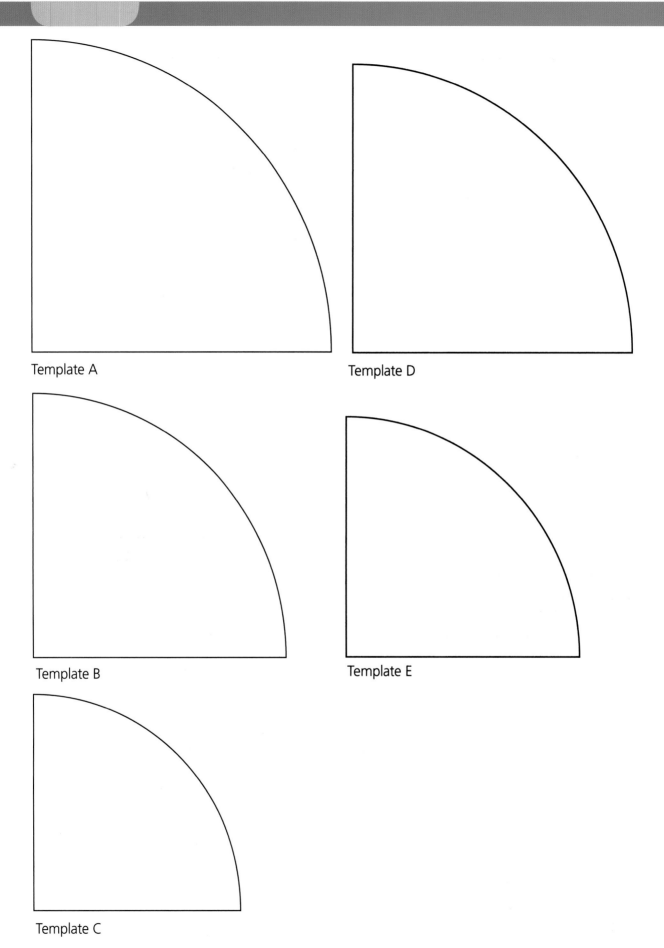

Template A

Template D

Template B

Template E

Template C

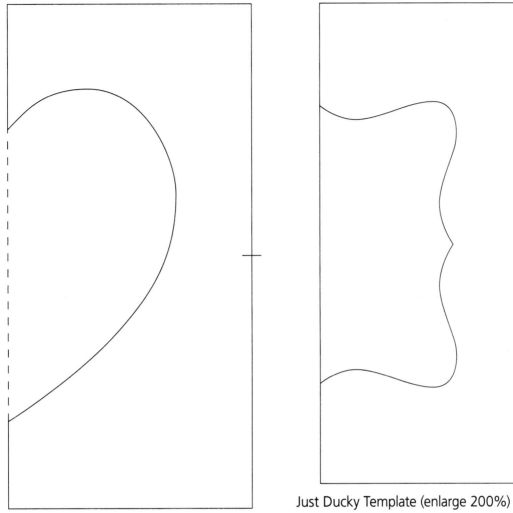

Sweet Hearts Template (enlarge 200% for Sweet Hearts project; leave as is for Basic Frame example on page 22)

Just Ducky Template (enlarge 200%)

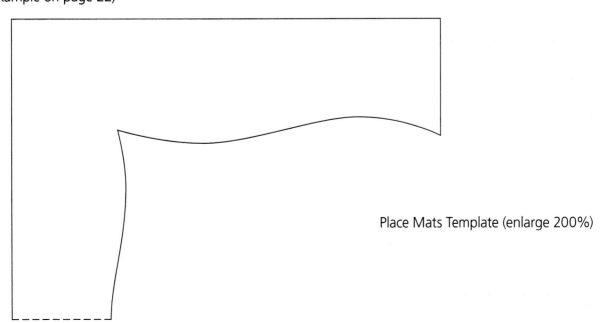

Place Mats Template (enlarge 200%)

Placement Guide

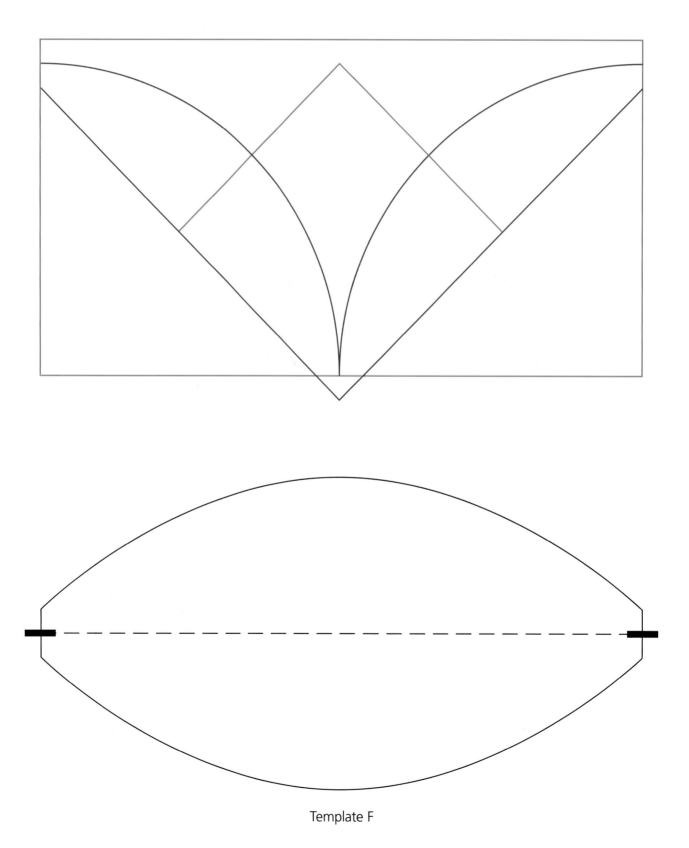

Template F

Resources

Wash-A-Way and Silk Threads

YLI Corporation
1439 Dave Lyle Blvd. #16C
Rock Hill, South Carolina 29730

Exam Table Paper

A-1 Medical Equipment & Supply Co.
134 31st Street
Ogden, Utah 84401
801-394-4455

Kai Pinking Shears

Shear Precision Scissor Co.
Item #N5350
P.O. Box 13671
Seattle, WA 98198
800-481-4943

Superior Thread Co.

87 East 2580 South
St. George, UT 84790
800-499-1777

Sixth Finger Stiletto

The Colonial Needle Company
Item #5715
74 Westmoreland Ave.
New York, NY 10606
800-963-3353
www.colonialneedle.com

Bias (self-adhesive)
⅜"-wide Straight, Adhesive Back Stay Tape

Professional Sewing Supplies
P.O. Box 14272
Seattle, WA 98114
206-324-8823

Johanne Moore

Riverside Quilting Services
73499 Sampson Lane
Pendleton, Oregon 97801
community.webshots.com/user/JoeyQuiltGirl
541-278-6824

Danetta Burnett

Quilt Crazy Custom Machine Quilting
Silvercreek, WA
mailto:quilt-crazy@quilt-crazy.com
www.quilt-crazy.com
360-985-0053

Fabric for Meloncholy provided by:

United Notions/Moda Fabric Corp.
Sunshine by April Cornell
13800 Hutton Dr.
Dallas, Texas 75234
800-527-9447

About the Author

Kathy Bowers lives and quilts in the state of Washington. She has self-published many patterns and teaches throughout the United States and South Africa. When she's not quilting, she enjoys spending time with her husband, Jim, her twelve grandchildren, and her great-grandson.

Get More Smart Stitching Tips for Your Money

Raggedy Reverse Applique
10 Fast, Fun and Forgiving Quilt Projects
by Kim Deneault

Discover a stress-free new appliqué technique in the detailed instructions and 175 color photos and illustrations of this book. Plus, an enclosed pattern insert includes patterns for all the projects—from the quick and easy to the more complex.

Softcover • 8¼ x 10⅞ • 128 pages
25 b&w illus. • 175 color photos
Item# Z0765 • $24.99

Sew It In Minutes
24 Projects to Fit Your Style and Schedule
by Chris Malone

Discover how to create each of the 24 projects in this book in 60, 90, 120, 240 minutes or less. Projects include ornaments, photo frames, appliquéd bib and more.

Softcover • 8¼ x 10⅞ • 128 pages
175 color photos and illus.
Item# Z0133 • $22.99

Sew Easy as Pie
by Chris Malone

Discover flavorful chapters filled with more than 12 easy-to-follow sewing designs coupled with delicious pie recipes. From cherry appliquéd tea towels and Almond Crust Cherry Pie to a pot holder with a pieced apple motif and Apple with Caramel pie recipe, there's a lot to love in this book.

Softcover • 8 x 8 • 144 pages
50+ b&w photos • 150 color photos
Item# Z0976 • $19.99

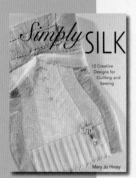

Simply Silk
12 Creative Designs for Quilting and Sewing
by Mary Jo Hiney

Uncover the mystery and diminish the fear of working with silk, and learn to transform this delicate fabric into a top choice material for all kinds of projects and techniques.

Softcover • 8¼ x 10⅞ • 128 pages
200 color photos
Item# Z0974 • $24.99

The Perfect Bag
101 Stylish Looks From Simple Patterns
by Linda McGehee

Discover through more than 150 step-by-step color illustrations and detailed design instructions how a multi-sized pattern can be used to create 101 different looks.

Softcover • 8¼ x 10⅞ • 128 pages
150+ color photos and illus.
Item# Z0318 • $24.99